Optimizing the
Financial Lives of Clients

HARNESS THE POWER OF AN ACCOUNTING FIRM'S
ELITE WEALTH MANAGEMENT PRACTICE

Optimizing the Financial Lives of Clients

Russ Alan Prince

Homer S. Smith IV, CFP, CRPC®,BFA™, CBEC™

Paul A. Saganey, CFP®

Important Disclosure

To Zita Prince

Who was always there for me.

Love, Russ

To Val,

For your unwavering support and encouragement.

Love, Homer

Jamie,

For giving me the opportunity to chase my 10X dreams
and unique abilities. I couldn't do it without you.

Love, Paul

HOUNDSTOOTH
PRESS

OPTIMIZING THE FINANCIAL LIVES OF CLIENTS

Harness the Power of an Accounting Firm's Elite
Wealth Management Practice

ISBN   978-1-5445-3458-9   *Hardcover*

       978-1-5445-3459-6   *Paperback*

       978-1-5445-3460-2   *Ebook*

Contents

Foreword

WHAT DOES IT MEAN TO BE ELITE?

The truth is, it is not for everyone. When I first heard about this strategy, I assumed—like you did, when you picked up this book—that it was just like every other tool, formula, and scheme that we have spent our careers trying to ignore—and then spent our careers examining and testing.

For every book with a good idea, there is a library full of bad ones littering our offices, our closets, and our minds. I was cautiously optimistic when I was first introduced to the folks at Integrated Partners in October 2018. I was skeptical because fifteen years ago, a different financial advisory firm approached us about the idea of providing financial products to our clients. Like most partnerships with financial advisors, it didn't take off the way we had envisioned.

The elite wealth management process that Paul, Homer, and the Integrated team designed helped us package wealth management in a different way. They provided support, brought in a team of experts, and helped us find opportunities to deliver great value to our clients.

There is an elegant simplicity in how this method builds better and deeper relationships with our clients. Armed with a wealth management partner and an elite mindset, we could do more for the client. We could help optimize their financial lives by giving them more.

As a result, we've grown. We've increased our wealth management revenue, and we've also increased our accounting revenue annually.

The process works because Integrated worked with us every step of the way. They gave us the tools, pressed us to grow, and directly helped us get there.

Delivering exceptional value to clients is the top priority. Everything else in this process, this method, and this book drives us back to that. By always maintaining the highest ethical standards, by delivering value as opposed to selling, and by delivering solutions from the basics to those that are state-of-the-art can make being elite simple.

In the end, to understand what "elite" is and why it works, you need to understand what it isn't. This isn't about us or about wealth management. This is all about doing the very best job possible for clients. This is growth. This is elite.

Joshua J. Bodenstadt, CPA
Partner in Charge, San Diego
Duffy Kruspodin, LLP

Introduction

HAVE YOU EVER LIFTED the hood of your car and checked the engine? It's okay to be honest; no one else is listening. The truth is, most of us have no idea what is happening under the hood. We confidently put our key in the ignition each morning, press the gas, and go.

When the check engine light comes on, sometimes we need to roll up our sleeves, take out the toolbox, and get to work. Occasionally, when we take out the toolbox, we are shocked to realize we don't have the right tools for the job at hand.

Running a business requires us to update our toolbox, because it's anything but simple. There is no check engine light. There are a lot of moving pieces under the hood that require the right time and attention to thrive.

How do you find the right tools and the right process to take your business to the next level? Well, you've already taken the first step: you've picked up the manual, this book. This book is designed for managing partners of accounting firms to help you deepen client relationships and grow their businesses by adding an elite wealth management division.

You've worked harder. Now it's time to work smarter. It's time to take your business to the next level. It's time to find the right partner, develop recurring revenue, offer more services, and uncover additional opportunities.

The time is now to follow a process to becoming elite. By following the time-tested process, we lay out in the pages ahead, you will be able to deliver a broader range of skills and services to everyone from complex business owners and family office clients to the mass affluent and retirees.

This will help contribute significant revenue to your bottom line. An elite wealth management practice regularly results in your accounting firm providing considerable additional accounting firm services to clients. You will have the confidence to approach the most demanding and complicated clients with the knowledge that you are backed by a team of tenured specialists, tackling all challenges as one.

As an accountant, you are always at the center of everything. But now, you'll be surrounded by valuable resources and support. Dive in and see how adding to your toolbox can position your business for long-term success.

CHAPTER 1

This Methodology is NOT for Most Accounting Firms

BEFORE DIVING INTO the material, take a moment to consider the following questions.

1. *Are you a managing partner or on the management committee of an accounting firm?*
2. *Do you want to deliver significantly greater value to your clients?*
3. *Do you have or are you interested in establishing a very successful wealth management practice?*
4. *Do you want to substantially accelerate the success of your accounting firm?*
5. *Do you want more high-quality clients for not only your wealth management practice but other practices at your accounting firm?*

If your answer to these questions is "yes," then the methodology we will be explaining for building and growing an elite wealth management practice may be right for you. There is no question that if you are the managing partner at an accounting firm, and you want to do the best job possible for your clients as well as meaningfully grow your firm, a well-run wealth management practice can be foundational to getting both these outcomes.

An Elite Wealth Management Practice

Accounting firms are professional services firms. They generally provide accounting and assurance services, and certain forms of tax expertise. Many accounting firms have expanded into other areas such as consulting, valuation, and talent recruiting. An area where a sizable and growing percentage of accounting firms are increasingly focusing on is *wealth management*.

To be clear, not all accounting firms are providing or will even consider providing wealth management. It proves to be a good fit for some firms, but not others. When it is part of a well-thought-out accounting firm's strategy, wealth management can be instrumental in delivering greater value to clients, which is the *number one objective*. The wealth management practice can also be instrumental in substantially increasing revenues and, thus, the value of the firm.

When the wealth management practice is elite—which we will explain in detail in the following chapter—your accounting firm benefits from a firm-wide multiplier effect. The promise of an elite wealth management practice includes:

- This is always the highest priority.

- These revenues are not only due to the substantial monies you earn by delivering financial strategies and products. An elite wealth management practice regularly results in your accounting firm providing considerable additional accounting firm services to clients.

- There will also be more revenue because the combination of technical expertise and the Everyone Wins Process will likely produce a pipeline of new high-quality clients.

An elite wealth management practice can—without question—be instrumental in substantially growing an accounting firm. You can become a hero to clients, the accountants at your firm, and even to other professionals, such as attorneys and bankers.

There is a caveat, and it is a big one. All the multiple advantages of an accounting firm's elite wealth management practice are a function of strategically building the appropriate version for each particular firm which includes mastering the Everyone Wins Process.

To date, while many accounting firms have established wealth management practices, only a small percentage of them have achieved anything close to their potential. Relatively speaking, very, very few of them can be considered *elite*.

Caveat

Just as an elite wealth management practice is not appropriate for all accounting firms, our methodology is NOT appropriate for all accounting firms with wealth management practices. What we will be explaining is NOT at all how most wealth management practices of any kind operate.

In our methodology:

- The client always comes first.

- The accountant and the accounting firm come second.

- The elite wealth managers and the elite wealth management practice come in a distant—far distant—third.

This ordering is a function of the core principles—the philosophical basis of the methodology—which we will discuss in the next chapter.

While our approach is completely focused on delivering greater value to clients to help optimize their financial lives, it also puts the accountant and the accounting firm center stage. Our methodology can easily give most accounting firms a serious competitive advantage, translating into considerably more business of every kind.

Again, the methodology is NOT for most accountants and accounting firms. Over the years, we have had pushback from accountants who preferred an easier, less demanding approach. We told these accountants if they find an easier approach that produces the same outcomes as the one we use, to please share it with us. We are only interested in what works best and will happily change gears. So far, *no* accountants have been able to show us an approach that even comes close to delivering the same level of value to clients, or can help tremendously grow an accounting firm.

If, however, our methodology makes sense to you, and you devote the time and resources, your accounting firm will likely get an exponentially better set of outcomes than the efforts made by accounting firms that have attempted to establish and grow a wealth management practice.

One action you might want to consider before going forward with wealth management is an internal assessment—what we call a practice profile.

Complete a Practice Profile

By a "practice profile," we mean a thoughtful evaluation whereby you and senior management develop an accurate understanding of your accounting firm's current strengths, weaknesses, opportunities, and any impediments to its success when it comes to building and growing a wealth management practice. If possible, it is usually best to complete this with the full partnership involved.

In our experience, the most successful accounting firms establishing wealth management practices—let alone elite wealth management practices—have aligned all the resources and support of the firm's partnership. If everyone agrees on the strategic vision, implementation becomes comparatively straightforward.

The first task is to check on the readiness and commitment of the partners at the accounting firm to being in the wealth management business. At that point, the critical questions are:

- Should the firm be in the wealth management business?

- Do the partners want to have a wealth management practice?

- What concerns do the partners have with wealth management?

- If wealth management is the way to go, do the partners want to level up to elite wealth management?

- What is the best way to deliver elite wealth management?

The clients of the accounting firm: In helping senior management at accounting firms decide if elite wealth management makes sense in their situations, one of the places we look at is the accounting firm's client base. This is regularly where most accounting firm wealth management practices get their initial clients.

It is very important to realize that the current clientele is not the whole picture. If you have an elite wealth management practice, accountants will regularly get more referrals to new high-quality clients. After going through discovery—explained in Chapter 7—we are able to get a good sense of the short-term growth that is possible from the new high-quality clients that are likely to be referred to the elite wealth management practice.

When thinking about these clients at your accounting firm, be aware that your elite wealth management practice is most likely appropriate for specific clients:

- Usually, the greater the business complexity, the more value your elite wealth management practice can bring. Business owners, for instance, have a range of interests, from dramatically lowering income taxes to putting in place succession or exit plans. These are matters that can be adeptly handled by your elite wealth management practice.

- Not only when clients' professional lives are complicated, but when their personal lives are complicated, does your elite wealth management practice shine. Helping to deal with the intricacies of extended blended families, for example, is something that your elite wealth management practice can skillfully address.

- A very likely deliverable of your elite wealth management practice is investment management and wealth planning. These services and the Everyone Wins Process result in clients being better informed so they can make smart decisions about their money.

By evaluating the wealth management potential within your accounting firm's clientele, you can quickly approximate the possible revenues over the next one to three years from incorporating an elite wealth management practice. This can give you a good sense of the worth of an elite wealth management practice, and such information is useful when considering the main business model options described in Chapter 5.

The partners of the accounting firm: Another important aspect of the practice profile is determining the degree to which a wealth management practice or an elite wealth management practice is supported by the accounting firm's partners. The more the partners are on board, the more success you will have.

Being on board is more than agreeing that an elite wealth management practice, for example, is a good idea. Preferably, the partners have to be willing to work with the elite wealth managers to identify opportunities, and then make sure the financial lives of clients are indeed optimized to the greatest extent possible.

For many accounting firms, what is helpful is going partner by partner and systematically identifying clients who would probably benefit from elite wealth management. When elite wealth managers go through this process with accountants, new opportunities are regularly uncovered for the accountant, and—very importantly—the elite wealth management initiative is tightly aligned with the accountant's interests. We address this matter in Chapter 8. Moreover, in accordance with Core Principle #3—which we'll detail in the following chapter—they have to be willing to stay involved.

In the course of the exercise, you may discover that your accounting firm is not ready or well-suited to establish an elite wealth management practice. We just want to reiterate...elite wealth management is NOT the right answer for most accountants and accounting firms. If you presently have a wealth management practice, you may find that it is NOT the best time to level up to elite.

If, on the other hand, your objective is to have an elite wealth management practice, there are specific steps you can take to move in that direction. To reiterate, we recommend this book for accounting firm managing partners who are strongly interested in doing a lot more than delivering financial strategies and products to clients. It is about the promises of elite wealth management:

- Optimizing the financial lives of clients
- Generating significant revenues for several accounting firm practice areas, including elite wealth management
- Having your accountants and elite wealth managers introduced to many more new high-quality clients

If you conclude that an elite wealth management practice or any type of financial services practice is NOT right for your firm, there are still very effective ways to upgrade the offerings of your accounting firm, thereby delivering greater value to clients and generating more revenues tied to financial strategies and products. Put another way...although your accounting firm would not be directly delivering the financial strategies and products, your accounting firm can still substantially generate more income and get more new high-quality clients. In effect, you can still work to optimize the financial lives of clients, which often includes restructuring your accounting firm's fee models to reflect the greater value you are providing.

Conclusions

This book is for you—a managing partner at an accounting firm—if you have or desire to establish an elite wealth management practice. We are talking about an elite wealth management practice as opposed to a wealth management practice. There is an extremely large difference between the two, which we will explain in the next chapter.

Herein, we will be detailing a mindset and a framework that—first and foremost—works to optimize the financial lives of clients. Our methodology also produces considerable revenues for most accounting firms across several different practice areas.

So there is no confusion...

- Yes, elite wealth management can be a powerful way to deliver significantly more value to clients.

- Yes, elite wealth management can easily become a 10X (or more, usually much more) revenue growth generator for many accounting firms.

- Yes, elite wealth management is NOT for most accountants and accounting firms.

You are going to have to decide if elite wealth management is a practice that makes good sense for your accounting firm. In making that decision, we recommend you take a hard look at your firm's strategy, resources, and limitations. This will probably lead you to first decide if you want to deliver financial strategies and products.

If you decide providing financial strategies and products is viable, you will still need to decide if wealth management is the right framework. One further question/decision...is elite wealth management the approach that will work well in your accounting firm?

The methodology we use has proven extremely effective. It is not what most wealth managers or your peers have likely seen. It takes commitment and work. The outcomes are exponentially greater than what most wealth managers at most any firm are producing. As we explain the methodology, you will need to decide if it will work for you and the accountants at your firm.

Central to our methodology are four core principles—the topic of the next chapter.

CHAPTER 2

Core Principles of Accounting Firm Elite Wealth Management Practices

EVERYONE HAS A business philosophy, whether they can precisely explain it or not.

1. *What is your business philosophy—your "why"?*
2. *What are the core principles of your business philosophy?*
3. *How immutable are your core principles?*

The way we think about accounting firms delivering wealth management expertise is not in line with most professionals. While many professionals are somewhat loose with their terminology, we are very specific about what we mean when we talk about an elite wealth management practice—which we will detail in the next chapter.

In thinking about elite wealth management, the place to start explaining our methodology is the unquestionable, fundamental core tenets of an accounting firm's elite wealth management practice. These four core principles are NOT in any way malleable or debatable.

The four core principles are:

- **Core principle #1:** The primary goal of an elite wealth management practice is to help optimize the financial lives of clients.

- **Core principle #2:** Elite wealth management is ALL about delivering exceptional value.

- **Core principle #3:** The accountant is always central when working with clients.

- **Core principle #4:** Elite wealth management is woven into the fabric of the accounting firm.

All these core principles interrelate. We will now go deeper into each one.

Core Principle #1
The Primary Goal of an Elite Wealth Management Practice is to Help Optimize the Financial Lives of Clients

Think of it this way . . . the goal of your elite wealth management practice is NOT to generate more revenues for your accounting firm. When we say this to accountants and wealth managers, so many of them immediately stress and tune us out. They want to sell financial strategies and products because that is how they make their money.

We are not saying the accounting firm's elite with management practice will not end up providing financial strategies and products, but that is not the goal. With elite wealth management, providing financial strategies and products is the way to help optimize the financial lives of clients.

What we strongly advocate is that an accounting firm's elite wealth management practice must be ALL about providing a sleeve of expertise that helps optimize the lives of clients. There are often a plethora of large and small ways elite wealth management can make the lives of clients a great deal better. All actions, all recommendations, and all analyses must be focused on helping deliver superior results.

As you can conclude, this orientation is not at all characteristic of a lot of wealth managers. Many wealth management practices are focused on selling financial strategies and products. At the same time, many wealth managers are themselves limited in what they can deliver. In contrast, your accounting firm's elite wealth management practice can access most all viable financial strategies and products to consistently deliver superior results to clients.

While we just said that the goal is not to generate revenues, the nature of elite wealth management will likely consistently produce remarkable direct revenues for your accounting firm. By being singularly focused on helping clients optimize their financial lives, your accounting firm's elite wealth management practice will likely turn out to be exceedingly profitable. The revenues your elite wealth management practice will produce take four forms:

- While this is not the goal, your elite wealth management practice will often find ways to add exceptional value to clients by delivering financial strategies and products.

- Our methodology identifies more than just wealth management possibilities. As clients likely have a diverse set of needs, wants, preferences, and concerns, our methodology helps identify these possibilities, thereby setting the stage to introduce other practice areas.

- Your elite wealth management practice will, in the course of working with clients, help these clients identify and introduce new high-quality clients. Consequently, there will be new high-quality clients for your elite wealth management practice, as well as other firm practice areas.

- Your elite wealth managers, in dealing with other professionals, will help them succeed. Consequently, very likely they will send your elite wealth management practice a steady stream of new high-quality clients. This is the norm, because your elite wealth managers are proficient with the Everyone Wins Process, discussed in Chapter 7 and expanded on in Chapter 9.

If your goal is simply to make a little more money selling financial strategies and products, an elite wealth management practice is not for you. You can certainly add wealth management to your accounting firm's offerings, and you will likely increase revenues. But this is a far cry from the considerable benefits you can deliver and achieve with an elite wealth management practice.

If you are deeply concerned about doing a sensational job for your accounting firm's clients and want to generate significantly more revenues—which will constantly happen by default—then an elite wealth management practice is likely the right way to go.

Core Principle #2

Elite Wealth Management is ALL About Delivering Exceptional Value

While most wealth managers talk about delivering value, in reality, they are often more absorbed in selling financial strategies and products. From where we stand, there is a monumental difference between selling financial strategies and products, and delivering value. Many wealth managers and other professionals do not recognize the difference.

To put it another way, elite wealth management and selling do not mix. And elite wealth management does not mix with "convincing," "persuading," "influencing," "motivating," or any other way of saying "selling."

Selling entails persuading someone to purchase something, in this case, financial strategies and products. Elite wealth management is about determining the latent needs, wants, aspirations, and concerns of clients. Then, the financial strategies and products that are most appropriate to help clients optimize their lives are introduced.

Not selling will prove to be one of the most consistently powerful advantages of your accounting firm's elite wealth management practice. The ability to understand the complexities of the worlds of clients, and use financial strategies and products to help them most effectively optimize their financial lives, enables your accounting firm's elite wealth management practice to add value in ways that make an enormous difference.

To avoid any confusion, if you are looking for your wealth management practice to sell financial strategies and products, then our methodology is most likely not for you. Similarly, if you end up partnering with a wealth management firm that is about selling financial strategies and products, the approach we are advocating is not for you.

On the other hand, if you are all about doing the best job possible for clients, our methodology will not only empower you to help optimize their financial lives, but your accounting firm will probably do exceedingly well economically. It is important to make sure all the accountants at your firm understand that elite wealth management is all about delivering exceptional value, and selling is completely off the table.

Core Principle #3
The Accountant is Always Central When Working with Clients

Some wealth managers look to accounting firms as a source of clients. They are looking for accountants to *hand off* their clients to them, so they can sell financial strategies and products.

At the same time, in some accounting firms, the accountants readily *hand off* their clients to wealth managers. After they make the hand-off, these accountants tend to go back to their practices, leaving the wealth managers to independently work with their clients.

While this is a very common practice, it can easily and often result in the clients being poorly served. This approach usually conflicts with the first core principle. Our methodology is very different.

The success of your accounting firm is a function of the value your accountants provide clients, and the quality of the relationships your accountants have with those clients. It is commonly recognized, and our research studies over thirty-plus years confirm, that accountants are the most cited trusted professionals by all manner of entrepreneurs, physicians, celebrities, corporate executives, and inheritors. Since accountants have a central place in the financial lives of their clients, it makes perfect sense to maintain—if not expand—these trusted relationships.

Always, the client is the client of the accountant. The accountant best understands the client, and has built a solid relationship based on delivering value. One of the aims of elite wealth management is to further enhance these relationships, often leading to more business and referrals to new high-quality clients. This is only possible as long as the accountants stay involved.

As we have been saying, elite wealth management regularly leads to opportunities for accounting firms to deliver additional services from other practice areas. For example, to accurately determine the amount of life insurance needed for a buy/sell agreement, a valuation of the company may be in order. There are a plethora of times when accounting and tax expertise are needed to correctly deliver the right financial strategies and products. Only when the accountant is integral to delivering wealth management expertise are these opportunities most likely to be realized.

We are not saying that accountants have to be at every meeting between their clients and the elite wealth managers. We are not saying that accountants have to be an expert concerning all the financial strategies and products. We are saying that accountants have to be involved throughout. We are saying accountants have to be in the loop when their clients are working with the accounting firm's elite wealth managers.

To be clear, when the accountant is involved throughout, there is a much, much higher probability of...

- Clients optimizing their financial lives

- Clients being very satisfied with the process and outcomes

- Business getting done, including producing additional accounting firm revenues

- New high-quality clients being referred

A major advantage of elite wealth management is that it opens the doors to new high-quality client referrals. By using the Everyone Wins Process, your accounting firm's elite wealth management practice will systematically facilitate being introduced to new high-quality clients. When these doors are opened, the accountant must be involved. The best way to think about this is that it is not just the elite wealth manager who is being referred; it is also the accountant and the accounting firm.

If the accountants at your firm are not interested and willing to be involved in working in concert with the firm's elite wealth managers, you will probably never reach the potential that is possible with an elite wealth management practice. More importantly, you are most likely in violation of the first core principle. It is unlikely that your accountants are helping their clients effectively optimize their financial lives.

Based on a great deal of success working with accounting firms to help clients optimize their financial lives, we can say it does not take much effort and time for accountants to be involved, thereby ensuring clients are getting superior results. When it comes to elite wealth management, accountants regularly have an oversight role that involves staying close to clients to confirm everything is working well. Still, it entails some effort and time, but the outcomes for all are always worth it.

Core Principle #4

Elite Wealth Management is Woven into the Fabric of the Accounting Firm

In part derivative of the previous core principles, elite wealth management is best not thought of as a stand-alone practice at your accounting firm. In many accounting firms, the wealth management practice is "over there." It is somehow attached, but not *really* part of the accounting firm. In our methodology, your elite wealth management practice is another way your accounting firms can better serve clients.

If your accounting firm's wealth managers are "over there," "a different part of the firm," or anything else that segregates them from and lessens their connection to the accounting firm, and the goal to add exceptional value to clients, the odds of being able to address the often-diverse needs and wants of clients decreases rapidly.

Elite wealth management is not a stand-alone practice, nor is it ancillary. To do the best job possible for clients, and get the most benefits for your accounting firm, elite wealth management is integrated into the thinking and philosophy of the accounting firm. It is not an afterthought. It is NOT something you want your accountants trying to cross-sell. Remember: elite wealth management is about delivering exceptional value; it is never about selling.

When elite wealth management is part of the fabric of your accounting firm, all the advantages we have addressed are very possible. This requires that your accounting firm's wealth management practice achieve elite status—and we will explain how to do this in the next chapter. It also requires the accountants to completely embrace the other three core principles.

The way elite wealth management practices become woven into

the fabric of accounting firms is often a combination of education and experience. Education covers a lot of ground, from understanding the difference between wealth management and elite wealth management, to how various financial strategies and products work *for clients*—not necessarily how they work but how they work for clients. We have repeatedly found that when accountants experience the benefits produced by elite wealth management—for clients, for themselves, and their accounting firms—they become strong advocates of our methodology.

If you are thinking of your accounting firm's wealth management practice as a subsidiary or something of the sort, chances are you will get some positive results, but odds are the results will be limited, if not nominal. You will probably be helping some clients and the accounting firm will be making some money, but you will most likely not be doing anything near optimizing the financial lives of your clients, or coming close to maximizing the economic benefits to your firm.

In contrast, if you want to optimize the financial lives of your accounting firm's clients and—because it will then happen—make a major positive difference in the revenues and growth of your accounting firm, elite wealth management needs to be blended into the composite solution set your accounting firm provides.

To integrate elite wealth management into the firm, there must be a champion. This is an accountant overseeing and advocating for elite wealth management within your accounting firm. That champion is YOU. In larger accounting firms, there usually need to be two champions: you and another accountant who is taking a more hands-on approach.

Conclusions

Take a moment to think about the four core principles:

- Is optimizing the financial lives of your accounting firm's clients your number one concern?

- Are you comfortable with the idea of NOT selling?

- Would the accountants at your firm be amenable to staying involved with their clients as elite wealth managers are brought in?

- Are you willing to work to integrate elite wealth management into the way your accounting firm operates and serves clients?

You need to answer all these questions in the affirmative if you want to get exceptional results for clients, your accountants, and your firm.

The philosophical foundation of our methodology is these four core principles. They underpin the effectiveness of elite wealth management. As we have cited, the advantages of an elite wealth management model are numerable, with the most important one being optimizing the financial lives of clients.

To reiterate, there are other ways than the methodology we use to bring financial strategies and products to clients. We do not want to "convince" you that elite wealth management is right for your firm, or that our methodology is the best way to deliver financial strategies and products to clients—see Core Principle #2. Our aim with this book is to provide you with a solid overall understanding of elite wealth management and how it can work in an accounting firm.

Your job is to determine if elite wealth management—as we are explaining it—is right for you and your accounting firm. You might conclude that our philosophy and methodology are not a good fit. Or, that some of what we say would work for your accounting firm, while skipping over other aspects. In the end, it is your decision.

We have been discussing elite wealth management without actually defining it. Having set forth the four core principles, we now turn to an explanation of elite wealth management.

CHAPTER 3

What is Elite Wealth Management?

YOU ARE THE MANAGING PARTNER in your accounting firm. You have or are evaluating what a wealth management practice means to your firm. You are also trying to determine how to get the greatest value from a wealth management practice. Can you comfortably answer the following questions?

1. *What is wealth management?*
2. *What is elite wealth management?*
3. *Which is a better solution for your accounting firm?*

If you have any uncertainty about the answers to these questions, know you are in good company. "Wealth management" is bandied about so easily by so many professionals and discussed at industry conferences, in the boardrooms of private client firms, in trade and mainstream articles, and before clients. But the term is, in fact, quite hard for the greater majority of professionals to define with any degree of precision.

Further complicating the conversation is the distinction between elite wealth management and wealth management. They are not the same. As we will see, the distinction is not semantics, but the ability to consistently deliver exceptional value to clients. The difference is also apparent when it comes to revenues.

Defining Wealth Management

The common definition...

Wealth management is providing financial strategies and products to clients.

Most definitions of wealth management emphasize "financial strategies and products." Financial strategies cover areas such as income, estate, and asset protection planning. It also tends to include the different types of qualified retirement plans and non-qualified deferred compensation. Financial products are often investments in a portfolio, life insurance, and credit.

Yes, financial strategies and products are central, and they are the way wealth managers are compensated. However, they take a distant second place when it comes to elite wealth management (see below).

An often-inconvenient truth of the wealth management industry is that ALL financial strategies and products are commodities. Without question, some financial strategies and products are better than others. But being better—even significantly better—does not make them unique. In one way or another, what one elite wealth management practice can provide, another elite wealth management practice can also deliver.

There are no financial strategies and products an elite wealth management practice can deliver that are inherently propriety. We have repeatedly run into situations where wealth managers, or other types of professionals, are pitching supposed unique financial strategies and products that only they can deliver. This is quite comical. Very quickly, we can either find the same source, or another, for the supposed proprietary financial strategies or products, or a comparable match to what they are offering.

This situation becomes especially facetious when the supposed unique financial strategy or product is being delivered by an external expert, such as a trusts and estates lawyer, or an actuary tied to a third-party administrator. The reason for the inappropriate comedy is that just about anyone can go to this professional, another high-level trusts and estates lawyer, or another talented actuary, and obtain their services.

To be clear, some financial strategies and products are more or less exclusive. This does not mean that they are unique. It is just that, in some cases, only certain wealth managers have access to them. For example, there are some very sophisticated defined benefit plans enabling business owners to put away a lot more money, with much of it going back to them. These qualified retirement plans are not unique, but they are not all that well-known.

Even though there are no unique financial strategies and products, the truth is that many self-proclaimed financial advisors and wealth managers are limited in their offerings. This can be a function of:

- The restriction and gaps in their wealth management platform
- The weaknesses in their wealth management team
- Knowledge limitations, such as a lack of awareness of more sophisticated financial strategies and products, which is quite common
- Their decision NOT to deal with certain financial strategies and products because of the time, effort, or complexity involved in the implementation

Getting right down to it, a relatively small percentage of wealth managers can deliver the full spectrum of state-of-the-art financial strategies and products. For many clients, their inability to provide bright-line, cutting-edge financial strategies and products is not a problem. A great many clients simply would not benefit from these financial strategies and products. In fact, in some cases, they would be deleterious.

On the other hand, do you want your accounting firm's wealth management practice to be able to deliver just about any legitimate financial strategy or product? If you want to be able to potentially optimize the financial lives of all your firm's clients as opposed to only some of them, you probably want to be able to deliver every viable financial strategy and product.

You need to decide if your wealth management accounting firm must be able to deliver state-of-the-art as well as basic financial strategies and products. In working with accounting firms, we find that the capacity to provide state-of-the-art financial strategies and products is very important, even if most clients do not need them.

If your accounting firm's wealth management practice is not—by design or otherwise—able to provide state-of-the-art solutions to clients, it cannot be considered elite.

Putting the Elite in Wealth Management

Being able to deliver state-of-the-art financial strategies and products *alone* does not, however, translate into elite wealth management. For us, elite wealth management is very straightforward...

Elite wealth management optimizes the financial lives of clients.

The only way to optimize the financial lives of clients is to be able to provide financial strategies and products from those that are considered basic to those that are state-of-the-art and do so because of a deep understanding of the needs, wants, dreams, and concerns of clients.

Technical proficiency is essential, but so is knowing the clients very, very well. Both capabilities are required for a wealth manager to be elite. We can see the difference in Exhibit 3.1.

Comparing Wealth Management to Elite Wealth Management

ASPECT	Wealth Management	Elite Wealth Management
Technical expertise	From basic to *potentially* state-of-the-art	From basic to state-of-the-art
Understanding of clients	Often limited	Always deep
Focus	Selling financial strategies and products	Optimizing the financial lives of clients
Collaboration	Tends to go it alone	Works in partnership with other qualified advisors

Exhibit 3.1

When it comes to being technically proficient, wealth managers have the basics covered, and might be state-of-the-art. In contrast, elite wealth managers can deliver any financial strategy and product. They cover the entire range of possible offerings, from the most rudimentary to the cutting-edge.

We recognize that many self-proclaimed wealth managers are far from technically proficient and are unaware of all the financial strategies and products. In one study for wealth managers, for example, we found that less than one out of twenty-five were knowledgeable about what financial strategies and products could be used to mitigate or eliminate the taxes on an investment portfolio. In another study of wealth managers, for about 70% of them, a 401(k) plan was the only type of qualified retirement plan they knew anything about.

Even when these wealth managers are familiar with and capable of implementing sophisticated financial strategies and using cutting-edge products, they are not necessarily elite. In these situations, there is a tendency for some wealth managers to "push" sophisticated financial strategies and products that eventually blow up. Even when there are no explosions, there is a good possibility that their recommendations will be seriously wrong for some clients.

A spectacular failure of a large percentage of wealth managers is that their knowledge of their clients tends to be limited. They might know the risk tolerance of a couple as measured by a questionnaire, but don't realize they have a special needs child. A wealth manager might know a client needs a succession plan for the family business, but fails to dig deeper, which would uncover the tension in the family over who would inherit the company, which is why no action is being taken.

While technically adept wealth managers are generally more focused on financial strategies and products, elite wealth planners are focused intently on assisting clients to optimize their financial worlds. This does not mean that technically adept wealth managers are not concerned with the interpersonal relationships and the psychology of their clients, but—from an objective standpoint—it is a much lesser concern, and they are much less knowledgeable about what matters to clients and what does not compared to elite wealth managers.

Uncovering what matters most to clients is crucial to helping them optimize their financial lives. There are processes, such as Everyone Wins, that can empower any professional to develop a deep, meaningful understanding of their clients. This extensive level of insight, combined with comprehensive technical capabilities, is what elite wealth management is about.

Very importantly, for the most part, wealth management is more often than not about selling financial strategies and products. Elite wealth management is about optimizing the financial lives of clients. While both use financial strategies and products, the difference is massive.

Elite Wealth Management Compensation Arrangements

While we have said that the objective of elite wealth management is to optimize the financial lives of clients, and that making money is a byproduct, that does not mean your accounting firm's elite wealth management practice will not be incredibly profitable, provided you pay some attention to managing the expenses.

The revenues you can earn by incorporating elite wealth management are probably a major consideration in your decision to build this practice area. Without question, the revenues from wealth management are often significantly greater than the revenues derived from other accounting practices. Then there are all the additional accounting revenues and the new high-quality clients your accounting firm will get because of your elite wealth management practice.

When it comes to elite wealth management, there are three main compensation arrangements. We find that most accounting firms' elite wealth management practices rely on a mix of the three. In different client situations, different fee arrangements are appropriate.

Advisory fees are sometimes charged by elite wealth managers for feasibility studies and other analyses, wealth planning, case design, and implementation. These fees can be hourly, retainers, or project-based.

Commissions are a function of providing certain products to clients. Traditional life insurance is commission-based. Moreover, in the case of life insurance, the commissions are statutory.

The greatest compensation for most elite wealth management practices is from **advisory fees,** where the accounting firm's elite wealth management practice is compensated based on the success of the strategy employed. In the field of wealth management, the most pervasive form of performance fees is asset-based fees.

You will need to decide on the right mix for your accounting firm's elite wealth management practice. For example, some accounting firms with elite wealth management practices sometimes structure client relationships where the advisory fees stay with the accountant, and commission and performance fees are credited to the elite wealth managers. At other accounting firms, all the revenue is booked by the elite wealth management practice.

There are protocols and even algorithms that can help determine how to divide the revenues. What we find very useful is to be flexible. The ability to adjust the compensation arrangements based on the nature of your clientele can make a big difference. Also, the ability to modify compensation arrangements for some one-off client situations is usually a good idea.

Elite Wealth Management is Not for All Accounting Firms

As we have stated, wealth management practices—let alone elite wealth management practices—are not good fits for all accounting firms. For example, at some accounting firms, more limited financial services practices are the better choice. Just being able to provide investment management or life insurance, as opposed to a broader array of financial strategies and products, is the better business decision. Let us also keep in mind that for many accounting firms, being compensated by providing financial strategies and products is a non-starter.

At the same time, it is important to realize that elite wealth management is not the best answer for all clients. Elite wealth management is most appropriate for wealthier clients. These are usually successful people, families, and businesses with more complicated situations, needs, and wants that would make elite wealth management a viable proposition.

Successful business owners, for example, tend to fit into this category. They are often looking for ways to mitigate taxes, deal with family concerns now and in the future, grow or sell their companies, and are interested in guidance on how to smartly handle their money. Elite wealth managers can assist a great many successful business owners in lowering their incomes and transfer taxes, as well as taxes on their investments. In some situations, they can help successful business owners purchase life insurance at a discount. All told, there are lots of ways elite wealth managers can add exceptional value to successful business owners.

Going back to the core principles, unless you see them as central, you will likely find that an elite wealth management practice is not the best way to go. Of course, your accounting firm can still provide financial strategies and products, but it will rarely reach the level of success that an elite wealth management practice will produce.

Conclusions

In an accounting firm, elite wealth management—while there may be a "testing period"—is a commitment. The idea that once the decision is made to establish and grow a wealth management practice money will start rolling in is a fallacy. Unfortunately, it's a fallacy we see surprisingly often.

You also must recognize that it often takes more energy and time to build an elite wealth management practice than a wealth management practice or a singularly-focused investment advisory or life insurance practice. A higher level of sophistication that is an elite wealth management practice necessitates more effort to make work. So, unless you and your partners are willing to commit, we suggest you *not* think in terms of elite wealth management. A wealth management practice where selling is the mantra is probably a better choice.

We did just say there can be a "testing period." In our experience, some managing partners are fairly quickly able to evaluate the advantages and obstacles to establishing and growing an elite wealth management practice. Some of them then tend to start putting the pieces together pretty quickly and move forwards fast. There are other managing partners, we have worked with, who are a little unsure. They have to see how an elite wealth management practice would work in their accounting firm before going all in.

If this is where you are in your thinking, we find that working cooperatively with an elite wealth management firm for a small number of selected clients will let you see the possibilities of building and growing an elite wealth management practice at your firm. This also allows you to see what it will likely take to establish and grow an elite wealth management practice. Thus, you will be able to make a more informed decision.

We now turn to a review of the four basic components of an accounting firm's elite wealth management practice.

CHAPTER 4

The Basic Components of Your Elite Wealth Management Practice

HAVING DECIDED ON BUILDING and growing an elite wealth management practice, you have to make some decisions:

1. *How are you going to ensure your elite wealth management practice is integrated into your accounting firm?*

2. *Which elite wealth management business model is best for your accounting firm?*

3. *How are you going to smartly grow your accounting firm's elite wealth management practice and generate additional accounting firm revenues?*

All your answers to these questions are interconnected. All are essential to making sure the core principles discussed in Chapter 2 are adhered to and that your elite wealth management practice is especially meaningful for your accounting firm.

Thinking conceptually, there are four basic components of your elite wealth management practice (Exhibit 4.1). Let us look at each of them.

The Basic Components	
1	Making Your Elite Wealth Management Practice Part of Your Accounting Firm
2	Your Elite Wealth Management Business Model
3	Mastering Process
4	Growing the Elite Wealth Management Practice

Exhibit 4.1

Making Your Elite Wealth Management Practice Part of Your Accounting Firm

Aside from having an accountant—you and possibly another partner—championing your elite wealth management practice, it has to be part of the strategic vision for your accounting firm. This is the only way it will be meaningfully part of your accounting firm, and not some sort of insignificant accessory.

There needs to be clarity of the partners' roles regarding the elite wealth management practice. Not only must expectations be clear, but the benefits of committing to making the accounting firm's elite wealth management practice succeed must also be quite clear.

If the rewards of the elite wealth management practice, for instance, are shared equally, irrespective of the contributions of the accountants, there is a higher tendency that some accountants will take the "free ride." At the same time, addressing their commitment to your elite wealth management practice can be part of their performance reviews.

Your Elite Wealth Management Business Model

There are different ways to deliver financial strategies and products. A lot of the decisions end up being based on the business model you choose. For example, in deciding on a business model, you are deciding the extent to which expertise is in-house or co-sourced.

Sometimes certain components of an elite wealth management practice are in-house, such as the elite wealth managers and administrative functions. Meanwhile, for most accounting firms, the answer lies in co-sourcing—which entails establishing strategic partnerships with elite wealth managers, infrastructure firms, and specialists.

Whether in-house or co-sourced, you need to make sure the accountants are always involved when it is their clients and that elite wealth management is well integrated into the way your accounting firm works on behalf of clients.

Mastering Process

Elite wealth management is a people business. Referring to Core Principles #1 and #2, elite wealth management is *all* about optimizing the financial lives of clients. Elite wealth management aims to deliver maximum value cost-effectively, and that commonly involves providing financial strategies and products.

There are powerful processes that enable elite wealth managers to develop a deep understanding of clients. These processes are instrumental in defining elite wealth managers, and critical to producing superior results for clients.

The process we use and will be diving into, in Chapter 7, is called Everyone Wins. When done well, the Everyone Wins Process provides the information and insights elite wealth managers use to determine and align the financial strategies and products that will best help optimize the financial lives of clients.

Growing the Elite Wealth Management Practice

Aside from defining success as doing the best job possible for clients, we are confident you want your accounting firm's elite wealth management practice to be profitable and to grow. There are highly efficacious ways to methodically grow an accounting firm's elite wealth management practice.

For most accounting firms, the first source of clients for elite wealth management is usually current accounting firm clients. To deliver exceptional value to clients, there are different ways the accountants at your firm can intelligently connect them with your elite wealth management practice. We talk about this in Chapter 8. This way, not only do the clients enormously benefit, but the accountants, the elite wealth management practice, and the accounting firm benefit as well.

To be clear, the accountants benefit because:

- They end up building stronger relationships with their clients.

- Wealth management, as well as substantial additional accounting practice and other revenues, are generated.

- New high-quality clients are introduced to the accountant.

Your elite wealth management practice will also grow as other professionals send over their best clients. Elite wealth managers, relying on the Everyone Wins Process, identify ways to add significant value to these other professionals. What is important to note is that adding value does not necessarily entail sending them clients.

An elite wealth management practice can give an accounting firm a major competitive edge. While always putting clients first, your elite wealth management practice can be a major way to grow your accounting firm by exponentially increasing firm revenues over time.

Conclusions

Yes, an elite wealth management practice can prove very rewarding for your accounting firm, aside from making a meaningful, positive difference in the lives of clients. What is required is not only doing what is necessary but doing it well. Here, we addressed the four basic components that can make your accounting firm's elite wealth management practice extremely successful, which, like everything else in the wealth management industry, are NOT secrets.

There are *no* secrets in the wealth management industry. There are *no* proprietary financial strategies or products. As such, what will make your accounting firm's elite wealth management practice extraordinarily successful is the ability to smartly and effectively put the four basic components in place and make certain the highest standards are always maintained.

If you believe your accounting firm, the accountants at your firm, and your clients would benefit from elite wealth management, it is wise to calculate the commitment you, your senior team, the partners, and other accountants and staff will need to make. You can adjust the levels of commitment, and sometimes taking an incremental approach to delivering elite wealth management is best. Still, a commitment has to be made.

In the next chapter, we will look at the five main different business models you can choose from.

CHAPTER 5

Selecting Your Elite Wealth Management Business Model

CENTRAL TO ESTABLISHING your accounting firm's elite wealth management practice is selecting a suitable elite wealth management business model.

1. *How familiar are you with the different accounting firm's elite wealth management business models?*

2. *From the vantage point of the accountants at your firm, what are the most important considerations in selecting a business model?*

3. *What is the risk/reward ratio you are comfortable with when it comes to your accounting firm's elite wealth management practice?*

A lot of thought goes into deciding first, whether elite wealth management is applicable and meaningful for your accounting firms; and second, if so, what the best way is to establish and grow an elite wealth management practice. The choice of business model makes a great deal of difference. There are five main business models to choose from.

One is not inherently better than another. The best choice of a business model is the one that is the best fit for your accounting firm.

Also, to some degree, you can mix and match the different business models, depending on circumstances. You can also transition from one business model to another based on your experience and the strategic direction you set for your accounting firm's elite wealth management practice.

Five Main Business Models

There are options—including internal, outsourced, and co-sourced models—that should be carefully evaluated against the human and capital resources of your accounting firm, and the overarching goals for your elite wealth management practice. It is important to realize that certain client situations may necessitate modifications to a selected business model. Here are five main ways to deliver financial strategies and products to clients (Exhibit 5.1).

Business Models	
In-source	Your accounting firm creates its own elite wealth management practice from scratch. The biggest obstacle tends to be recruiting the elite wealth managers.
Buy	Your accounting firm buys one or more elite wealth management firms.
Build then add	After building an elite wealth management practice, your accounting firm buys one or more elite wealth management firms or adds to the ranks by recruiting more elite wealth managers.
Co-source	Your accounting firm enters into a formal equity or revenue sharing joint venture with one or more elite wealth management firms.
Outsource	On a case-by-case basis, your accountants refer their clients to external elite wealth managers for predetermined compensation.

Exhibit 5.1

When considering which business model is most viable for your accounting firm, there are many variables to weigh. Factors affecting which business model your firm adopts include the cost of implementation and time to market. You will probably want to also take into account how well each option aligns with your accounting firm's culture, values, and way of doing business. Finally, you will likely need to take into consideration any initial and ongoing training requirements.

Let us address some of the major considerations at most accounting firms.

Fixed costs are high if you choose to build your elite management practice from scratch. Elite wealth managers are often expensive to recruit and retain. There are also ongoing educational costs so they can stay state-of-the-art. Specialists are usually outsourced, as we will discuss in the next chapter. However, if there is enough client demand, some specialists are brought in-house, which adds to the fixed costs.

When building an elite wealth management practice, most infrastructure costs can be outsourced, but there are still going to be some expenses. Many times, when accounting firms build an elite wealth management practice, they bring a percentage of the required infrastructure in-house, which can be very expensive.

Buying an elite wealth management practice can be even costlier, at least initially. Today, there is likely to be a large premium for the acquisition. As the wealth management industry is booming, the owners of wealth management firms are finding there are several different types of acquirers such as other wealth management firms, accounting firms, banks, and consolidators. This makes it even more of a seller's market as private equity pays top dollar for wealth management firms, thereby driving up prices everywhere.

If you aim to build an elite wealth management firm and then add on other elite wealth management firms or recruit more elite wealth managers, the fixed costs are usually high.

For many accounting firms using this business model, the idea is to use the profits from their elite wealth management practice to finance the additions. This strategy has the possibility of creating conflicts if the elite wealth managers end up questioning their compensation, as monies are going to add-ons and recruiting efforts.

Another potential complication is that sometimes the add-ons are not as successful compared to the elite wealth management practice the accounting firm built. If this is the case, the accounting firm has purchased some very expensive assets. It will therefore likely take some time before the accounting firm recoups its costs.

The fixed costs for co-sourcing are low, as the expenses are predominantly variable. For accounting firms, some additional personnel is sometimes required. Still, the operational costs are principally borne by the respective firms while revenues are shared. Similarly, outsourcing has little, if any, fixed costs.

Because of the considerable cost differentials among the business models, most accounting firms start with the co-source or outsource model; this lets the accounting firm's senior management and the accountants get a very good idea of what it takes to succeed in the wealth management business. A large percentage of accounting firms who adopt the co-source or outsource business models continue with that model, but some that have experienced success transition to one of the other business models.

Accountants are highly responsible for the clients they introduce to your elite wealth management practice across all five business models, as long as you are using the methodology we are advocating.

To remind you, Core Principle #3 is where the accountant is always involved and in charge.

The complication is that most accounting firms with wealth management practices are not adhering to the four core principles. If you consider the way most accounting firms are operating their wealth management practices, there is some degree of accountant responsibility for clients, but most of the time, clients are handed off by the accountants to the financial advisors or wealth managers.

Hand-offs will certainly result in some business getting done, but a great deal of business is almost always overlooked. At the same time, business for other accounting firm practices is also regularly missed.

Many times, the wealth management business is not seen, or disregarded, as the wealth managers only deal with what the client was referred for, such as investment management. These professionals fail to discern that the client would greatly benefit from a sophisticated defined benefit plan and a reshaping of business interests to protect assets from potential future unfounded lawsuits. Most certainly, because most wealth managers are siloed in their thinking, they will get few, if any, new high-quality client referrals.

Cultural alignment between accountants and wealth managers can be problematic. Generally speaking, the two professionals attract different personalities.

In all these business models, a high degree of cultural alignment can be ensured when both parties put the interests of clients first, as elite wealth managers are solidly focused on fostering the success of each accountant they work with. Elite wealth managers modify their approach not only to match the norms of the accounting firm but also to accommodate the personal preferences of individual accountants. Nevertheless, there still are times when differences occur. This is when you or the accountant you put in charge of the endeavor will need to help facilitate cohesiveness.

With appropriate attention to costs, the **profitability** of an elite wealth management practice can fairly quickly become exponentially greater than most other accounting practices. This is a function of the inherent profitability of financial strategies and products compared to time-based—or even project-based—compensation arrangements. The difference in profitability for the accounting firm by each business model is a function of the financial arrangements you establish, including compensation to the various professionals involved and your fixed costs.

Each business model can generate significant elite wealth management revenues. By using our methodology, which includes putting in place an elite wealth management practice, there will be considerably more total accounting firm revenues from current clients and new high-quality clients. You will probably find it very useful to think of your elite wealth management practice as a powerful revenue multiplier for your entire accounting firm.

Risk among interested parties. As with any new business initiative, the risk to your accounting firm must be mitigated. Each state has different rules and regulations, but in order to move forward, understanding each party's responsibilities and offsetting risk must be determined.

Future equity must be considered. At some point, one of the interested parties may look to sell their interest in the clients they are working with. Each of the business models addresses future potential equity in different ways. It's best to understand the financial implications with any business partner prior to beginning the relationship.

While not every business partner will offer this, some partners will share in the equity of the revenue stream.

Conclusions

It can be complicated to determine which business model to pursue. There are five main ways to establish your accounting firm's elite wealth management practice. Each has its advantages and drawbacks. What is detrimental to many accounting firms with wealth management practices is that their business model may not be in sync with their firm's culture and strategic initiatives.

As none of the five business models are inherently better than another, the best one for your firm is a function of several factors. We touched on six of these—fixed costs, accountant responsibility for the clients they introduce to your elite wealth management practice, cultural alignment, profitability, risk, and future equity. Without question, if you indeed establish an elite wealth management practice, a major financial consideration is how you choose to balance fixed costs with revenues; in other words, how much do you want to invest compared to the returns you want to achieve.

Using the co-source or outsource models is the way many accounting firms get into the wealth management business. These business models are mostly, if not entirely, variable cost models. Starting with the co-source or outsource models is a risk mitigation strategy.

Your elite wealth management team is central to your accounting firm's elite wealth management practice. Each of the business models "comes" with an elite wealth management team. Many times, an accounting firm's wealth management practices fall short of their potential, if not turn out to be major mistakes, because the wealth management team is far from elite. We will now discuss what makes a wealth management team elite.

CHAPTER 6

Ensuring You Have an Elite Wealth Management Team

BUILDING AND GROWING your accounting firm's elite wealth management practice hinges on a team composed of accountants, elite wealth managers, and other talented and capable professionals and providers working under close direction. In making sure you have an elite wealth management team…

1. *Are all the team members incredibly focused on supporting each other in delivering exceptional value to clients?*

2. *Do all the team members understand and operate by the four core principles?*

3. *Is there a deep bench of outstanding specialists available when needed?*

4. *Are the accountants with the elite wealth managers coordinating and overseeing ALL the specialists?*

5. *Would you be proud to introduce this new team to your best clients?*

All these questions need to be answered in the affirmative for the wealth management team to be considered elite. What we are talking about is majorly different from the so-called team approach pursued by many wealth managers.

In the team approach that is usually characteristic of the wealth management industry, the wealth managers have contacts with other experts they can refer to or that they can call upon to help address various client matters. Unfortunately, from the client's perspective, this approach is commonly very inconsistent, and sometimes even counterproductive. Also, the accountants usually play a subservient role, which only diminishes the value clients receive.

Characteristics of Elite Wealth Management Team Members

For each type of financial strategy and product an accounting firm's elite wealth management practice chooses to provide, it is necessary to have processes in place so that implementation is always precise. Since an elite wealth management practice can offer every legitimate financial strategy and product, it all comes down to the quality of the professionals involved. All these professionals must have certain characteristics:

- Integrity is always essential. All elite wealth management team members have to be scrupulously honest and reliable. There are no excuses for moral lapses of any kind. For instance, each wealth management team member must be willing to turn down business if a client wants to cross some legal or ethical line.

- In every way, such as responsiveness to inquiries and attention to detail, all elite wealth management team members embrace professionalism. Another example of professionalism is that elite wealth management team members are continuously learning, and some are even contributing to their area of expertise.

- There should be a strong level of comfort and appreciation among the members of the elite wealth management team. When elite wealth management team members recognize each other's talents and abilities, they are much more effective, with clients extensively benefiting.

- For an elite wealth management team to run smoothly, each member must understand his or her role, and the overarching role the accountants play. All too often, an assembly of high-powered, talented professionals can lead to conflict, as egos get rubbed the wrong way. Each elite wealth management team member must understand that the accountant who is introducing the client to the elite wealth management practice is ultimately in charge, in accord with Core Principle #3.

External experts are always part of an elite wealth management team. These specialists are brought in as needed, under the supervision of an elite wealth manager responsible to the accountant.

These external experts must be top-of-the-line experts in the fields. What matters is that the external experts who are members of the elite wealth management team are truly, technically outstanding. There can be no question that they are among the very best at what they do.

It helps majorly if the specialists are also thought leaders. It also is beneficial if some of your elite wealth managers are thought leaders.

Being thought leaders, these specialists share their knowledge and perspectives without reservation. Doing so validates their expertise, making it easier for your accountants to make introductions.

Incorporating External Experts into an Elite Wealth Management Team

Concerning all external experts, your accounting firm's elite wealth management practice has a negotiated mutually beneficial arrangement. The way the specialists work with the elite wealth management practice can be critical to success. The promise of elite wealth management is only possible when the compensation and working arrangements with each specialist are skillfully negotiated.

Most of the time, the elite wealth managers and possibly the accountants are responsible for sourcing, vetting, and negotiating arrangements with the specialists. Still, as the managing partner, you or someone on your senior team will often need to approve the selection and agreements.

As managing partner, you will—or designate someone to—negotiate the arrangements with external experts. You will likely be concentrating on three aspects:

- Each specialist needs to be appropriately compensated. At the same time, clients are looking to pay the least possible for the most value possible. It is up to you to strike a balance between the cost of the services provided by external experts and the value they deliver, and maintain the balance.

- Clients want to be able to jump to the head of the line. You, therefore, have to establish the arrangements so that when you need a specific specialist, that professional is readily available—if at all possible.

• As noted, all team members must recognize and agree that the accountants are running the show. They have to be willing to follow the accountant's lead, and agree to his or her decisions concerning his or her clients. Experience tells us that this issue needs to be reinforced regularly.

With the ultimate success of your elite wealth management practice being highly dependent on your elite wealth management team, you must make sure every team member is completely on board. Therefore, you or your designee would be wise to put effort into the negotiations with the specialists about their roles, their fees, and the working arrangements.

To maximize the value of your elite wealth management team, two considerations make a major difference when you negotiate:

• To get the most out of the negotiations, you need to understand how each professional makes money—not only how their firms make money but how they personally make money. This means you know how their business model operates, such as how the equity at their firms is shared, whether a particular professional is given origination credit and what that entails.

• Certainly, being compensated is high on their list of interests. But they have other interests as well. Operational arrangements such as workflow, for example, tend to be a factor that must be taken into consideration when working with external experts. Also, among many professionals, there is a psychological boost in working with certain types of clients, such as the ultra-wealthy. The more you know their interests, the more effectively you can negotiate.

Negotiating with external experts is usually a very fluid process. As your elite wealth management practice becomes more successful, the arrangements with the external experts will be adjusted. Meanwhile, there are likely going to be client situations where you structure one-off arrangements.

There are other issues when it comes to the specialists you will probably need to be on top of. For example, when troubles between specialists and clients arise, the accountant or the elite wealth manager must be there to resolve the issues. This is a "when" not an "if" occurrence. These troubles are less common and less intense when accountants are involved.

Another issue is making sure the specialists are paid. Very likely you or your elite wealth manager will be closely involved in helping to establish the fees that the specialists will charge each of your accounting firm's clients. Because you are helping set the fees, and because they are members of your accounting firm's elite wealth management team, you are also responsible for making sure the specialists are paid. You have to ensure all the professionals involved work together effectively and are fairly rewarded for their contributions.

Conclusions

Your elite wealth management team is foundational to building and growing an elite wealth management practice. The team is composed of accountants who are intent on bringing more value to their clients, elite wealth managers, external experts, and support staff. When the elite wealth management team is *elite* as we have defined it, the results for the clients and your accounting firm, as well as for all the team members, are usually incredible.

We have found that it takes effort to make sure your elite wealth management team is not only exceptionally technically proficient but also able to develop a deep understanding of clients and work together without their egos crashing the party. While you will likely not be constantly interacting with the members of your elite wealth management team, it can be helpful to be sure the members have the characteristics we discussed.

Having addressed the different elite wealth management business models and the importance of the elite wealth management team, we now turn to the process that makes a technically capable wealth management practice great—Everyone Wins.

CHAPTER 7

Mastering the Everyone Wins Process

THINKING ABOUT YOUR elite wealth management practice's ability to optimize the financial lives of clients...

1. *Can the wealth managers connect with clients on a very preferential and often deeply personal basis?*

2. *Can the wealth managers develop a meaningful understanding of each client's interests to most effectively provide him or her with financial strategies and products that produce superior results?*

3. *Can the wealth managers explain recommendations and advice in ways that strongly resonate with each client?*

Let us put it this way: If they cannot do these things, then they are not elite wealth managers. There is no question that the wealth management team must be highly technically proficient. Still, the ability to optimize the financial lives of clients, as well as build an extraordinarily successful practice, is—to a very large degree—dependent on the quality of the relationships between the accountants, the elite wealth managers, and clients.

The Everyone Wins Process is what makes a technically proficient, state-of-the-art wealth management practice into an elite wealth management practice.

The Everyone Wins Process

The Everyone Wins Process is a proven methodology for enhancing and maximizing business relationships (and usually personal relationships as well). The process is far from new. On the contrary, it probably goes back to when people had to first cooperate to survive. Put another way, the Everyone Wins Process is ancient and universal wisdom. It is solidly predicated on human nature.

In business, when it comes to enhancing and maximizing relationships, the most successful professionals are extremely systematic. Put another way, they have made the Everyone Wins Process central to the way they relate to others, including clients, other professionals, and staff.

There are two key concepts to the Everyone Wins Process:

- Clients, for example, are going to act in ways that they believe will get them the outcomes that matter to them. While this is a truism that few people have any issue with, most people do not act as if it is a fact.

- The answer is always about how to help clients achieve the outcomes they are looking for. Moreover, as we will discuss in Chapter 10, mastering the Everyone Wins Process can result in a steady stream of new high-quality clients from other professionals.

To be able to consistently deliver exceptional value, your elite wealth management practice must intensely focus on the goals, needs, and problems of every client they are introduced to. The elite wealth managers need to constantly make sure they are on the right track, as the wishes and concerns of clients are quite malleable and will readily change.

With the Everyone Wins Process, the elite wealth managers do NOT—as is common among most professionals—make the conversations solely about themselves, their practice, or their firm. They will never need to tell others how smart, capable, or talented they are. They will never need to tout the nature of their elite wealth management practice, or the competencies of the accounting firm.

Most of the time, focusing on themselves or the accounting firm is not the way to most effectively share with clients the exceptional value your elite wealth management practice or accounting firm can bring to them.

Besides, have you ever run into a professional who said something along the lines of "I'm not that good, but I'm working on getting better, and I try really hard?" We never heard a professional say anything of the sort, and we suspect neither have you. On the contrary, just about all the professionals we have met over the decades exalt their intellectual prowess and their technical proficiencies. Generally, they tend to pontificate about how good they are, how good their firm is, and so forth.

By making it all about clients or other professionals, your elite wealth managers can uncover their interests. Only then will they know how they can help them achieve their agendas—how they can deliver exceptional value. What commonly occurs is that when the elite wealth managers truly know the hopes and dreams, anxieties, and concerns of clients, your elite wealth management practice can help them optimize their financial lives.

In sum, for your accounting firm's elite wealth management practice to excel, a deep understanding of clients is required. This way, your elite wealth managers can customize everything they do to help each client accomplish his or her interests (provided it is within the law).

To repeat, the big difference between the most successful professionals, and those who are less successful but just as technically capable and determined, is often the quality of their client relationships. Furthermore, while just about all leading professionals are using the Everyone Wins Process at some level, the most successful ones are far more systematic in their approach. If your accountants, for instance, are presently not very systematic in building extraordinary relationships, they certainly can be.

There are many facets to the Everyone Wins Process. One facet, and the one we will be discussing, is the discovery process—"discovery" for short. Because of discovery, elite wealth managers develop a deep and meaningful understanding of their clients. Thus, they can determine the appropriate financial strategies and products, as well as how to best communicate the solutions to clients.

The Role of Discovery

The discovery process is a central component of the Everyone Wins Process. It is the way to learn about others. Generally, by using open-ended questions, people will share what is going on in their lives. To gain some perspective, in the case of many clients, the following types of open-ended questions at the beginning of a conversation tend to be very effective:

- How are things going with you and your family?
- How are things going with your business?
- What's the most important thing we should be discussing?
- What are you most concerned about?

There will almost always be a need to probe to get a deeper and more comprehensive understanding of what is occurring in the lives of clients, as well as what does and does not matter to them. Probes are just open-ended questions focused on a specific matter that is being discussed. Probably the most effective question (including variations) to use as a probe is...

Can you tell me more?

By prompting clients to go deeper in sharing their worldview and circumstances, the number of opportunities to deliver exceptional value increases dramatically. The following are some examples of probes:

Example 1:

- *Client*: The business has really taken a hit. Revenues are off more than 20%, and I'm not sure what I can do to get things back to the way they were before.
- *Elite wealth manager*: What steps are you thinking about to revitalize your company?

Example 2:

- *Client*: I'm very concerned about my kids one day inheriting my money. I don't think they're prepared to handle it.

- *Elite wealth manager*: What do you think might happen? What might each one of them do?

Example 3:

- *Client*: With all that's going on, I'm seriously thinking of selling the business. The numbers are good and likely to get better. I've been at this for decades, and no matter how hard I try, I can't get any of the kids interested in taking over.

- *Elite wealth manager*: What have you done so far to make sure you get the most for your business when you sell it and that you put the most money possible in your family's pockets?

Example 4:

- *Client*: My son is getting married, and I have serious reservations about the marriage. My wife and I are concerned about a large chunk of the family money disappearing in a divorce.

- *Elite wealth manager*: What actions are you or your son taking to ensure that the family money stays with your son or his children?

Probing means using open-ended questions to get a deeper and more expansive understanding of what clients have done, are thinking, and what they want. During the discovery process, it is wise to make ample use of probes.

The three rules of discovery: Discovery is not hard for most professionals to master. Nevertheless, doing discovery well means following three rules:

- Discovery is about learning the thoughts, ideas, beliefs, and so forth of clients and others. Frankly, it is very hard for wealth managers to do that when they are talking. If a wealth manager is doing a lot of talking, he or she is likely not to learn very much about the client. Elite wealth managers follow the 10% rule of discovery, which means they do not talk more than 10% of the time during a conversation if they intend to ascertain a client's goals and aspirations, concerns, and anxieties. If they are talking more than that, the client will probably not open up and share.

- So many professionals go into client situations with all sorts of presumptions. Sometimes, these presumptions happen because they were told something by other people before-hand, and sometimes these presumptions are misperceptions of the professionals. Either way, they are obstacles to under-standing what is truly important or not to clients. Embracing intentional ignorance means going into client situations consciously not knowing anything no matter what informa-tion is at hand, and learning from clients.

- Too many professionals do some form of discovery and think they have the answers, that they now know their clients. This is a serious fallacy. Elite wealth managers are constantly engaging in discovery with clients. Perpetual discovery always leads to a deeper, more meaningful understanding of clients. Also, as the lives of clients change over time, perpetual discovery lets elite wealth managers adjust financial strategies and products as appropriate.

What elite wealth managers are looking to learn during the discovery process: First and foremost, elite wealth managers are NOT trying to find out what financial strategies and products clients want or think they want. Besides, most of the time clients will not know.

A wealthy investor, for example, would like to not pay taxes on his growing investment portfolio. He will probably not know anything about possible ways to mitigate or eliminate these taxes. He just does not want to pay taxes, if doing so is legally possible. The responsibility of the elite wealth manager is to understand what he wants and to be able to show him viable options.

Another example is when clients want to sell their companies. There are various ways, such as using certain trusts, to lower the taxes they have to pay on the sale. Relatively few clients likely know of these possibilities. Instead, clients are looking to your accounting firm's elite wealth management practice to help them make wise financial decisions.

When elite wealth managers are learning about the interests of clients, their intent is NOT to quickly explain possible solutions. They do not jump into the conversation with answers. What they want to do is understand (Exhibit 7.1).

- Elite wealth managers need to know just what clients want to accomplish—their immediate goals and objectives, as well as their longer-term goals and objectives. Without this information, they cannot show how their advice, and recommended financial strategies and products, will help them achieve their agendas.

- It is self-evident that what matters most to clients are the matters they will most quickly address. Therefore, elite wealth managers are always looking for information that helps them understand the highest priorities of clients, which are predominantly their critical concerns. Knowing what has their attention gives elite wealth managers insight into their current and future actions, and possibly provides them with an awareness of the ways they can optimize their financial lives.

- This is about how clients see themselves, how they want to see themselves, and how they want others to see them. People, for the most part, will rarely take actions that conflict with their self-images. Embedded in their self-image are their strengths and weaknesses, as well as their anxieties and insecurities.

- Elite wealth managers not only want to know the thoughts and feelings of their clients, but also the basis of those perspectives and emotions. So, elite wealth managers look to identify the facts and attitudes clients are relying upon, and the experiences that underpin their viewpoints and actions. Included here are their unshakable beliefs.

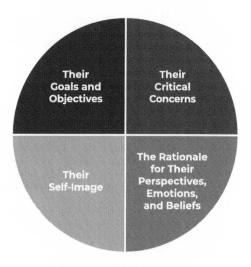

Exhibit 7.1

By and large, ascertaining the interests and concerns of clients, or anyone for that matter, is habitually the most complex part of determining which financial strategies and products are most appropriate. Getting to the most relevant facts and points of view takes persistence and a certain artistry. Regularly, elite wealth managers have to move beyond the surface and superficial answers. They have to dig deeper to determine what matters most.

Using the Everyone Wins Process with Other Professionals

Being introduced to new high-quality clients from other professionals such as attorneys and bankers is a way to substantially grow your elite wealth management practice, as well as other accounting firm practices. The Everyone Wins Process is extremely effective in creating a pipeline of new high-quality clients from other professionals.

There are two main aspects to the approach (Exhibit 7.2). The elite wealth managers employ the discovery process to learn all about these other professionals, ranging from the nature of their practices to their aspirations and concerns. Then, with these insights and information in hand, they add value, which commonly means helping them substantially grow their practices. When we say "substantially grow their practices," this does not necessarily include sending them clients.

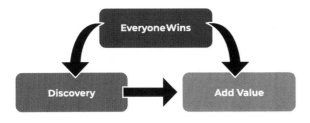

Exhibit 7.2

We will go into more detail about using the Everyone Wins Process with other professionals in Chapter 10.

It Is All About Delivering Exceptional Value

State-of-the-art technical competence, coupled with the Everyone Wins Process, is the quintessential approach to delivering exceptional value to clients.

In many ways, the approach is diametrically opposed to the way many professionals operate. This approach is in stark contrast to those professionals, including a very large percentage of wealth managers who concentrate on selling financial strategies and products. Instead, the Everyone Wins Process is all about clients or other professionals.

To emphasize the point, the Everyone Wins Process is...

- **Never** about selling or persuasion or influence
- **Never** about your elite wealth management practice or your accounting firm when working with clients or other professionals—unless they inquire
- **ALL** about finding opportunities to be caring and helpful
- **ALL** about helping optimize the financial lives of clients
- **ALL** about getting superior results for your clients and helping other professionals achieve their agendas
- **ALL** about delivering exceptional value

It is easy to spot professionals who take a self-centered or firm-focused approach to dealing with clients. Their conversations are all about what they can do and how good they are. No professionals we ever met have told us that they were "not really good." Quite a few have pointed out that they are one of the best in their respective fields. A few even proclaimed themselves the best. Most of these professionals have very pretty PowerPoints and brochures to go along with their proclamations, which are all about them and their firms.

When your elite wealth managers use the Everyone Wins Process, they are focusing intently and raptly on their clients. It is all about the clients. As your elite wealth management practice can deliver the spectrum of financial strategies and products from the basic to the state-of-the-art, very likely, the ultimate success of your elite wealth management practice is all about human connections.

One of the reasons the Everyone Wins Process is so effective is because most professionals want to sell their services or products, and work quite hard to make their offerings try to fit even when they do not. Consequently, many clients need honest, completely unbiased, excellent advice that will help them achieve their interests.

Considering the multitude of professionals doing a substandard job for their clients, mastering the Everyone Wins Process produces a considerable advantage over possible competitors for both accounting work and wealth management business.

Thanks to your elite wealth management practice, you are finding more ways to be a hero to the clients of the accounting firm and to the multitude of new high-quality clients the firm will be referred to. There will be times when the financial strategies and products your elite wealth management practice can provide do not fit. However, because most clients are looking for answers, powerful solutions, and direction, by helping them achieve their interests, your accounting firm will—over time—not only deliver considerable value to them, but you will usually massively benefit.

Conclusions

A great many wealth managers, while intending and possibly could do a great job for their clients, are often thinking more about themselves and their practices. Consequently, they are often acting in ways that do not deliver exceptional value to their clients. This is more a structural facet of the financial services industry than anything at all malicious. Nonetheless, it offers a marvelous opportunity for your accounting firm's elite wealth management practice.

The power of the Everyone Wins Process is deeply understanding the world of clients, as well as other people, such as attorneys and bankers. Elite wealth managers do this systematically by using the process of discovery, which operates through the skillful use of questions. When elite wealth managers engage in discovery, it is all about the other person. The insights and information they discern permit them to identify ways to add exceptional value.

By using the Everyone Wins Process, your elite wealth managers can connect in powerful ways other financial professionals simply cannot. Thus, they can produce superior results for the accounting firm's clients, as well as for other professionals who can provide the elite wealth management practice as well as the accounting firm with new high-quality clients. All in all, the Everyone Wins Process means your elite wealth management practice is better able to deliver exceptional value to clients, which also means much more business.

As noted, the Everyone Wins Process is also instrumental in building productive relationships with other professionals. To help these professionals build their practices, elite wealth managers must initially develop a solid understanding of their business models, their clientele, and their interests.

For many accounting firms, the clients of accountants are a major source of business for their elite wealth management practice. In the next chapter, we will discuss how we identify elite wealth management client opportunities.

If you want to learn more about the Everyone Wins Process, the book—*Everyone Wins! How You Can Enhance and Optimize Business Relationships Just Like Wealthy Entrepreneurs*—is available on Amazon.

CHAPTER 8

Identifying Elite Wealth Management Client Opportunities

FROM MANY MANAGING PARTNERS, we get the following questions:

1. *What should I do to get the accountants to identify clients for the elite wealth management practice?*

2. *What about educating accountants on financial strategies and products?*

3. *How do I make sure that the accountants are always involved?*

The methodology we use explicitly addresses all these questions in accordance with the core principles. There are ways to empower accountants and provide the appropriate education so we never deviate from Core Principle #3. Think of it this way:

- The elite wealth managers work with the clients of accountants to help optimize their financial lives.

- These clients will always be clients of the accountant.

- The value elite wealth managers bring to these clients strongly enhances the quality of the accountants' client relationships.

- The enhanced relationships lead to considerably more business and referrals to new high-quality clients.

Here is where our methodology and the approach most accounting firms with wealth management practices tend to deviate the most. We want to be completely forthright. As we said in Chapter 1, our methodology is not for most accountants or accounting firms. It is, however, extremely effective.

Another point: our methodology is not exclusive. For example, you can certainly add other approaches to your accounting firm's business development aside from what we are doing and recommending. These other approaches might accelerate the success of your elite wealth management practice. (If they do, please let us know.)

Not implementing our methodology, however, might very well limit your accounting firm's and wealth management practice's ability to optimize the financial lives of clients. You might very well also find you have put a ceiling on revenues and growth, when otherwise, not even the sky's the limit.

Discovery with Accountants

To get your accounting firm's elite wealth management practice generating considerable business, fast and ongoing, you'll likely have to start with the clients at your accounting firm. Let us be very clear: this is just a starting point. As we discuss in Chapter 10, because of the methodology, your elite wealth management practice will be referred to new high-quality clients, who will also likely make use of other accounting firm practices.

Certainly, some accountants will send clients over to the elite wealth management practice because the client asks them to. The conversation goes something like this:

- *Client*: I need an investment advisor. Don't you have some relationship with an investment advisor?
- *Accountant*: Come to think of it, I think we do...Yes, we do.
- *Client*: Can you connect me?
- *Accountant*: I think so.

Okay, maybe the conversations are a little better than this one. But we know firsthand that many of them are not, and a good percentage are worse.

Elite wealth managers make it as easy as possible for accountants to identify the clients who are likely to get exceptional value from the elite wealth management practice. The elite wealth managers will also show accountants how to make the proper connections.

The way this works best is when elite wealth managers go through the discovery process with each accountant. The result is that the elite wealth managers understand:

- The value each accountant brings to his or her clients
- The way each accountant is growing his or her practices
- The clientele of each accountant
- The career trajectory and aspirations of each accountant
- The way they can significantly help each accountant grow his or her practice

This version of discovery is the same version the elite wealth managers use with other types of professionals, such as attorneys and bankers, and is discussed in Chapter 10.

With these insights into the professional world of an accountant, elite wealth managers can help open doors to clients who would get enormous benefits from elite wealth management. The insights also give the elite wealth managers the guidance they need to help accountants meaningfully grow their practices outside of connecting clients to the elite wealth management practice.

One of the objectives of elite wealth managers, for example, is to develop and implement a bespoke business development capability for each accountant where elite wealth management plays a supporting role. Therefore, in-depth knowledge of an accountant's practice is essential. Also, by knowing how particular accountants prefer to work, elite wealth managers can customize the way they work with them and their clients to get the best outcomes possible.

Strategic scenario sessions: A variation of discovery with accountants is the strategic scenario session. This is when an accountant and elite wealth managers evaluate client fact patterns. This approach allows the professionals to spot where the elite wealth management practice, or some other accounting firm practice, can add tremendous value (Exhibit 8.1).

The following steps can be helpful when conducting strategic scenario sessions:

Strategic Scenario Sessions

STEP 1	Specify the interests and concerns of clients, and collect relevant materials:	Elite wealth managers always need to know what is meaningful to particular clients. Often, it is also necessary to collect relevant materials. For example, if a client is focused on making sure their loved ones are taken well care of if he or she were to die, all sorts of specific information are needed. If possible, his or her current estate plan is collected for review.
STEP 2	Brainstorm elite wealth management, as well as other possible solutions:	The elite wealth management team and the accountant brainstorm possible solutions. Sometimes, other accountants from different practice areas are brought into the sessions or consulted. During these sessions, there are no constraints on feedback. Everyone is encouraged to offer opinions and share ideas, even if these thoughts are still germinating.
STEP 3	Determine the most appropriate solutions:	Among all the possibilities, some solutions will stand out. Sometimes they will involve the elite wealth management practice, and sometimes they will not. The very best ideas, approaches, financial strategies, products, and accounting firm services the group comes up with are the ones presented to the client.
STEP 4	Decide how to present the best solutions:	The accountant with input from the group decides how to communicate the most appropriate solution. Commonly, the experts who know the presented solutions best are involved in these client meetings to address concerns and answer questions.

Exhibit 8.1

Concentrating on delivering exceptional value to clients tends to produce spot-on results fairly quickly. The best way—and in our opinion, the only way to do this—is by having the accountants involved throughout the process.

We are not discounting the role education can play in helping accountants identify elite wealth management client opportunities. Lectures on the working of financial strategies and products, for instance, can for many accountants be quite useful. The complication is that such an approach does not regularly lead to accountants connecting the financial strategies and products to the needs, wants, and preferences of their clients. On the other hand, showing that accountants know what to look for usually produces greater results. For some accountants, combining both approaches is best.

Educating Accountants on Situations to Watch For

Over the decades, in working with numerous accountants and going through the discovery process—resulting in understanding their goals, their practices, and their clientele—we have repeatedly found many opportunities for adding value to clients. For perspective, the following are some high-probability client situations.

For all of the following high-probability client situations, we first point out what the accountant can watch for. Then, we identify the likely problems and some potential solutions. In each of these examples, we have also included a question that can be used as a probe to get more details, and potentially spark action.

Watch for	Problem	Potential Action	Probe
Clients with pools of assets that the accounting firm's elite wealth management practice are not investing.	The accounting firm's elite wealth management practice does not have, or has only a portion, of the client's investable assets.	Implement an asset capture strategy	"How happy are you with your current investment returns?"

Watch for	Problem	Potential Action	Probe
Clients with highly concentrated stock positions.	Lack of diversification	Create a well-diversified investment portfolio. Sell positions using charitable trusts. Employ various hedging strategies.	"Are you comfortable with such a large percentage of your wealth in a single stock?"

Watch for	Problem	Potential Action	Probe
Clients with special needs children.	Ensure the care and treatment of these children no matter what.	Establish special needs trusts. Structure an investment portfolio to address the child's current and future income requirements. Acquire life insurance.	"Have you taken all the steps possible to make sure Robert is financially secure?"

Watch for	Problem	Potential Action	Probe
Clients with outdated estate plans.	An estate plan does not provide the resolution the client wants.	Review the current estate plan, and if there are gaps, make modifications. 1035 exchange of the life insurance or write a new policy.	"If you could have the same life insurance coverage for less cost, would you be interested?"

Watch for	Problem	Potential Action	Probe
Clients with teenage children driving vehicles titled in their parents' names or owned by the parents' company.	If the child is in a car accident where someone is injured or killed, the parents may be liable.	Select trusts or corporate structures to shield the assets of the parents. Maximum liability insurance.	"If your son hits a bus full of pre-school children and someone on the bus is badly hurt or killed, the lawsuit may cut right through your umbrella policy, and everything of value you own may be lost. What do you want to do?"

Watch for	Problem	Potential Action	Probe
Clients with teenage children driving vehicles titled in their parents' names or owned by the parents' company.	If the child is in a car accident where someone is injured or killed, the parents may be liable.	Select trusts or corporate structures to shield the assets of the parents. Maximum liability insurance.	"If your son hits a bus full of pre-school children and someone on the bus is badly hurt or killed, the lawsuit may cut right through your umbrella policy, and everything of value you own may be lost. What do you want to do?"

Watch for	Problem	Potential Action	Probe
Clients that own businesses and have equity partners.	Ownership of the business goes to someone the remaining partners do not want to work with, such as the deceased's spouse.	Have an up-to-date buy/sell agreement funded by investments or life insurance.	"Do you want to be in business with your partner's spouse?"

Watch for	Problem	Potential Action	Probe
Clients with assets that produce an income stream that continues after death, such as intellectual property.	Creates a taxable event for heirs, as the total value of the asset will possibly be subject to estate taxes.	Structure the estate so that the value of the income stream is preserved for the client's loved ones. Acquire life insurance to pay the estate taxes.	"Do you care if the government gets 40% or more of the value of your patent when you die instead of your family?"

Watch for	Problem	Potential Action	Probe
Clients who are at risk for divorce.	A case of fraudulent conveyance may occur if the assets are moved at the wrong time.	Redo the client's estate plan while the couple is still together. Prenuptial agreements, or the use of trusts, to hold assets pre-divorce. Use of select asset protection strategies in advance of divorce.	"Are you interested in some ideas to keep your money out of the hands of that gold digger?"

Watch for	Problem	Potential Action	Probe
Clients with a foreign-born spouse.	Certain estate planning strategies do not apply.	Ensure all the wealth planning takes into account all relevant tax scenarios, such as multiple citizenships.	"Unless you use a particular type of trust, your heirs will lose half your estate to the IRS. Do you know the type of trust you used?"

Watch for	Problem	Potential Action	Probe
Clients who plan to sell their companies.	The value of the company is expected to increase, resulting in the need to one day pay more in estate taxes.	"Freeze" the value of the business.	"Are you interested in saving more than $xx million in future estate taxes?"

While these types of elite wealth management and accounting firm opportunities proliferate, the real world is usually a lot messier. However, after discovery with accountants, this can be a great way to start.

Because of this approach, many times there will be a need for other services your accounting firm can provide, aside from elite wealth management. In this last example, there might very well be the need for a valuation of the company, or a quality of earnings report.

While these are fairly common situations, how each one is managed can be very different. Moreover, the potential actions we cited are very basic. There are ways of accomplishing these results that tend to be more sophisticated. It will all depend on the specific circumstances and interests of the clients involved.

We have found that many accountants initially are overwhelmed, or find it difficult, to "watch for" these and other client situations. What they soon realize is that many, many, many fact patterns repeat. As you likely concluded, these client situations are quite common. Moreover, many of the possible actions repeat as well. The elite wealth management opportunities we cited are prime examples of this.

Repeat situations are more likely the case when you are dealing with specific client cohorts. For example, with successful business owners, some high-probability situations are:

- Lower incomes taxes

- Transferring the business to heirs or selling the company

- Mitigating risks—especially catastrophic risks

Another common scenario is when successful business owners want to maximize their incomes in retirement. The solution set includes various types of qualified defined benefit plans and non-qualified deferred compensation alternatives.

Celebrities with loan-out corporations, for example, have specific needs and wants, and can use the structure to address some of them. There are some financial strategies and products that, combined with loan-out corporations, can be extremely effective in dramatically lowering tax bills.

Accountants need to realize that client fact patterns will repeat, and repeat, and repeat. Oftentimes, there will be the ability to address the needs, wants, and preferences of these clients by using the same financial strategies and products. On the other hand, from innovations to changing tax environments, there will be scenarios in which different financial strategies and products produce better outcomes. Elite wealth managers can take each client's fact pattern and deliver exceptional value.

Tax season: Another advantage to educating accountants on high-probability client situations is they will likely find a plethora of opportunities for elite wealth management during tax season. For most wealth managers, tax season is a time when accountants vanish. We recognize that tax season is a great time to find ways to later help clients optimize their financial lives and grow an elite wealth management practice.

We have found that accountants can easily add a few questions to their conversations with clients during tax season. The clients tend to readily answer the questions, and their answers indicate potential elite wealth management opportunities to follow up on when the intensity of tax season abates.

Conclusions

Accountants have relationships with clients, and by delivering additional exceptional value to their clients because of the accounting firm's elite wealth management practice, they can build stronger relationships with their clients and substantially grow their practices. Put another way, the involvement of the accountants is a requirement in our methodology.

There are many ways to help accountants identify elite wealth management client opportunities. We recommend you consider all sorts of options, as you know the accountants at your firm best. Still, we have had, and continue to have, enormous success by using the Everyone Wins Process.

When elite wealth managers engage in discovery with accountants, all manner of client opportunities are uncovered. A version of discovery called a strategic scenario session can be very useful in finding ways to help optimize the financial lives of clients.

When accountants understand what to look for, and not just how financial strategies and products mechanically work, they tend to more easily identify elite wealth management client opportunities. For those accountants who want to learn more about the mechanics, education needs to be made available. For the accountants who have a lesser interest in the mechanics, they will still likely need to understand the fundamentals of the financial strategies and products. These accountants usually choose to learn when client possibilities arise.

In the next chapter, we look at how elite wealth management is provided where the accountant is always involved.

CHAPTER 9

No Handoffs to the Accounting Firm's Elite Wealth Management Practice

HAVING IDENTIFIED WEALTH MANAGEMENT client opportunities, accountants must be able to bring in the elite wealth managers. This leads to a few questions...

1. *What is the best way to introduce the accounting firm's elite wealth management practice?*

2. *What is the best operational strategy when it comes to accountants and elite wealth managers working together on behalf of clients?*

3. *How involved does the accountant have to be?*

Going back to Core Principle #3, the last question is easy to answer. The accountant is always involved. The extent of that involvement is a function of the nature of the client and the requirements of the situation.

It is All About Outcomes

You likely do not want to take medicine. However, you likely very much want the benefits of the medicine. Along similar lines, clients do NOT want financial strategies and products. They want the benefits of financial strategies and products. They want outcomes.

In the wealth management industry, the emphasis is, mistakenly, almost exclusively on technical proficiencies. Again, you have to always remember, your elite wealth practice has all the possible financial strategies and products clients might need. Many times, this is possible because of the specialists on your elite wealth management team.

If your elite wealth management practice does not have a particular financial strategy or product at its fingertips, getting a comparable one or—after some networking—being able to access what is required is usually fairly easy. So, being able to provide appropriate financial strategies and products is never a serious obstacle.

Just as important and many times more valuable is truly understanding the interests of clients. Elite wealth managers, having mastered the Everyone Wins Process, really understand what clients want to accomplish, and because of your elite wealth management team, they have both the **what** and the **how**. All too often, many professionals do not really understand the needs, wants, and preferences of clients, for they are too wrapped up in the how—the technical wizardry they are very good at.

Elite wealth managers understand the value of discussing outcomes with clients. Many times, at least initially, they have to help accountants do the same. This means that accountants do not say to a client anything like, "You should talk to our wealth managers—they can help you." Regrettably, these kinds of introductions are very, very common and often ineffectual. The following four steps are a framework for constructively connecting clients with your elite wealth management practice:

Focusing on Outcomes

STEP 1	We addressed this topic in the previous chapter. Whether clients come to them with a straight-out request for an introduction or the determination is due to discovery between elite wealth managers and accountants or the accountants recognize a particular fact pattern, it is evident that certain clients can benefit by being introduced to your elite wealth managers.
STEP 2	The accountant—sometimes with the assistance of the elite wealth manager—determines the motivations of the clients. For example, a couple is concerned that the family monies will be lost due to their child marrying a gold digger. Another example is a client who is anxious about being caught up in unfounded lawsuits.
STEP 3	The accountants confirm the outcome the clients are looking for. For the couple fearful of losing family money, the outcome is making it as impossible as possible for an in-law to walk away with the family monies. For the client who worries about lawsuits, the outcome is to insulate assets.
STEP 4	At this point, the clients are quite interested in how the accountants can help them. The accountants can then introduce the elite wealth managers as resources with the solutions that will give them their desired outcomes.

Exhibit 9.1

We have found that some accountants initially see this process as too demanding. In the field, accountants usually find it ends up being a lot simpler than it sounds, and a very natural way of working. Usually, all accountants need is some experience with the approach. Moreover, your elite wealth managers, through discovery, will regularly facilitate the process, taking away much if not all of the stress the accountants might be feeling.

No Handoffs, Ever

Many accountants might find a viable prospect for their accounting firm's wealth management practice and send him or her over. The accountant will then move on, focusing on other clients. In effect, the accountant handed the client off to someone else.

This approach does indeed work some of the time. However, we often find the approach works in opposition to the larger agenda of delivering exceptional value to clients and growing the accounting firm. It violates Core Principles #3 and #4.

The best way to build your elite wealth management practice, as well as your accounting firm, is for accountants to stay involved with their clients. Being involved does not mean they are intensely involved all the time. But they do indeed have to be involved at some level.

These accountants do not have to be at every meeting, nor do they have to be experts in wealth management. What it does mean is that the accountants are the gatekeepers and the conduits between the clients with whom they have a solid relationship, and they have other capabilities within your accounting firm, including wealth management.

When there are handoffs:

- Clients can get multiple messages, and those messages are often not aligned. When the accountants are involved, and therefore talking to the elite wealth managers and clients, they can make sure misunderstandings are avoided.

- When the accountants are not involved, even when the elite wealth managers are identifying additional accounting firm services for these clients, there are many times follow-through is lacking, and opportunities are missed.

- When the accountants are involved, they regularly get new high-quality clients. When they are not involved, this happens, but it happens comparatively rarely.

In our methodology, the client is *always* the client of the introducing accountant. To ensure the relationship between the accountant and the client intensifies because of elite wealth management, the accountant always needs to stay involved.

An Example of How Accountants are Always Involved

To get a better idea of how an accountant is always involved, consider the following example.

In going through discovery with an accountant, the elite wealth manager identifies some successful small business owners who are very interested in lowering their income taxes. They have already taken all the possible deductions as well as some other steps. Even so, they might be able to deduct hundreds of thousands, and in some cases possibly over a million dollars, by adopting a sophisticated defined benefit plan.

With the opportunity identified, the accountant or a staff member collects the requisite data, which is usually easy to do. The information will let the elite wealth manager analyze to determine if one or more of the different types of sophisticated defined benefit plans are viable.

What does not happen is the accountant goes to the small business owners to discuss the possibility of saving a lot of money by substantially lowering their income taxes. If one of the sophisticated defined benefit plans is not viable, having discussed it with the small business owners is more likely than not going to annoy them. The prospect of paying fewer income taxes sounding great, only to be told the financial strategy is not applicable for them, is not going to strengthen the accountant's relationship. It will probably be a detraction.

After doing the analysis, the elite wealth manager will go over the results with the accountant. Only then is the decision made whether to bring the financial strategy to certain successful small business owners. As there are always going to be pluses and minuses with any financial strategy, with the number in hand, it is up to the accountant to decide which successful small business owners to talk to about sophisticated defined benefit plans.

If the decision is to show some successful small business owners how they would benefit from such a benefit plan, meetings are set. Even though the objective is to share the analyses with the small business owners during these meetings, the elite wealth manager will conduct discovery with them first, to make certain there are no more pressing concerns.

If, for instance, some small business owners say they plan on selling the company within a year or so, then the sophisticated defined benefit plans are likely off the table, and the discussion will shift to what will it take to prepare the company for sale so it can be sold at the highest possible price.

If, after discovery, the small business owner is focused on mitigating income taxes, then the discussion will include a sophisticated defined benefit plan. If they decide to move forward, the elite wealth manager will implement the plan while the accountant will oversee the process and make certain the expectations of the small business owner are being met.

When small business owners implement these sophisticated defined benefit plans, because of the Everyone Wins Process, the accountant and the elite wealth manager can reliably expect some referrals—usually at least two—new high-quality clients for elite wealth management and other accounting services.

Conclusions

The accountants are not only central to identifying elite wealth management client opportunities; they are critical to realizing the promise of elite wealth management for clients, your elite wealth management practice, and your accounting firm. Therefore, they are involved throughout.

By discussing interests and concerns with clients, your accountants will readily be able to introduce clients to your elite wealth management practice. In the beginning, this process tends to be facilitated by your elite wealth managers. But as the accountants get some experience and see the positive results, they will most readily become adept fairly quickly.

What is so telling about our methodology is that the clients feel their accountants are doing them a great favor when they introduce them to your elite wealth management practice. Consequently, the rapport between the accountants and their clients increases. Also, more business, as well as new high-quality client referrals, are inevitable.

No question, no debate: There are *no* handoffs from accountants to the elite wealth management practice. We have made a very big deal of this. It is a central tenet of our methodology. If you or your accountants are not in agreement with this core principle, we recommend you look at other approaches to provide financial strategies and products.

In the next chapter, we examine ways you can grow your accounting firm's elite wealth management practice beyond the clients of your accountants.

CHAPTER 10

Growing Your Elite Wealth Management Practice Beyond the Clients of Your Accountants

HAVING BUILT AN ELITE wealth management practice...

1. *How interested are you in substantially growing it?*

2. *How interested are you in growing it beyond the clients of your accountants?*

3. *Do you currently have systematic processes in place to significantly grow your elite wealth management practice?*

Most likely, the answer is "yes" to the first two questions, and "no" to the third question. Delivering more value to clients, and bringing in new high-quality clients, is a given with our methodology.

We never want to be solely dependent on growing an accounting firm's elite wealth management practice with only the firm's clients. However, to get the results we say you will, you have to think in terms of a few years as opposed to a few weeks or months. It takes time to grow an elite wealth management practice, and success is majorly dependent on optimizing the financial lives of clients.

There are several strategic initiatives you can put in place to grow your elite wealth management practice, and we will talk about a few of them. First, let us review how most accountants get new clients.

How Accountants Get New Clients

While there are many exceptions, according to decades of empirical research, most accountants get most of their new clients from referrals. These referrals generally come from current clients.

We refer to the approach as "waiting for the phone to ring." There are four steps to waiting for the phone to ring:

Waiting for the Phone to Ring

STEP 1	An accountant does a great job for a client.
STEP 2	That client is approached by someone looking for specific services.
STEP 3	The client connects what the person is asking for with what the accountant can deliver.
STEP 4	The client then might—let us emphasize "might"— refer this other person to the accountant.

Exhibit 10.1

Getting referrals this way is all dependent on someone the accountant's client knows, who wants what the client understands is just what the accountant can deliver. As most clients have a siloed or limited view of what their accountants do, lots of opportunities are missed. Still, even when the mental connections are made, the accountant's client has to be inclined to make the referral. There are lots of places along this chain where client referrals derail.

Further complicating getting referrals is that the accountant's clients—even those who are elated with the outcomes they achieved—are very likely not often talking about their accountants. When their accountant's clients talk to others, it is not surprising that most of the time is spent talking about family, their business, their jobs, or what is going on in the world. The professionals they use do not come up that often unless someone is complaining or questioning and looking to make a change.

An elite wealth management practice is proactive in fostering client referrals. Furthermore, these are all high-quality, highly desirable clients.

Facilitating High-Quality Client Referrals

In large part, by using the Everyone Wins Process, your elite wealth managers better understand the world of their clients. Indirectly, they are also ascertaining whom these clients can refer.

Through the discovery process, the elite wealth managers learn the business and personal ecosystems of each client. There is a real good chance that some of these other people would make excellent clients for the elite wealth management practice, or other accounting firm practices. Determining whom these clients can refer is pretty easy.

Think of a successful business owner, for example, who has been a client of yours for more than five years...

- What are the names of the suppliers to his or her business?

- What are the names of the customers of the business, if those customers are other businesses?

Using the discovery process, the elite wealth managers uncover the interests of the accomplished entrepreneurs, including the other businesses they deal with. Elite wealth managers rarely ask for a referral at that moment. Instead, they put together a list of all the companies and the owners their business owner clients deal with. Not only are the elite wealth managers identifying potential future clients, but they are also gauging the level of rapport their business owner clients have with these other business owners.

One easy and unobtrusive way to help determine the quality of these relationships is by looking at how long the two business owners have been doing business together. Generally speaking, the longer the relationship, the more likely a well-framed referral to your elite wealth management practice will be seriously considered.

At the appropriate time, the elite wealth manager helps their clients make introductions to specific business owners to whom they are close. The way they ask makes all the difference. In this context, the accountants and elite wealth managers get the best results when they ask in a manner that focuses on the proven exceptional value they have delivered. Consider the following 4-step process (Exhibit 10.2).

Learning about whom clients have strong relationships with, and who can also benefit from your accounting firm's elite wealth management practice, is eminently doable. It sometimes takes a little more finesse to map out the relationships of clients who are not business owners. This approach regularly results in current clients giving a fairly comprehensive list of all the other people they know, as well as indicating their ability to refer them.

The Elite Wealth Management Approach to Getting Referrals from Clients

STEP 1	The elite wealth management practice does a great job for a client.
STEP 2	The elite wealth manager has determined some successful business owners of other people the client knows well.
STEP 3	The elite wealth manager—using questions—works with the client to determine whom to introduce.
STEP 4	The elite wealth managers help the client make the introduction by providing context and framing.

Exhibit 10.2

Build a Pipeline of New High-Quality Clients from Other Professionals

What proves to be the most effective way to garner new high-quality clients for your accounting firm's elite wealth management practice is to be introduced to them by other professionals, such as lawyers and bankers. Moreover, if the objective is to move upmarket, the likely best way to connect with wealthier clients is from referrals from other professionals whom they are currently engaging.

To get the best referral results possible from other professionals, your elite wealth managers need more than a relationship with them. They need these professionals to be advocates. By deftly applying the

Everyone Wins Process, these professionals can become advocates and will introduce your elite wealth managers to their best clients (Exhibit 10.3).

Relationships with Other Professionals Compared to Advocates

Relationships with Other Professionals	Advocates
Periodically, a client will be referred.	Consistently, these professionals introduce their best clients and actively lobby on your elite wealth manager's behalf.
Your accounting firm's elite wealth management practice is one of a number of firms that the other professionals are considering.	Your accounting firm's elite wealth management practice is the only or primary firm for the other professionals' best clients.
The predominance of the opportunities will be driven by the clients of these professionals.	These other professionals are vigorously looking to make introductions of their best clients to your accounting firm's elite wealth management practice.
The other professionals rarely follow up with their clients after providing a referral.	The other professionals strongly follow up with the clients they referred to your accounting firm's elite wealth management practice.

Exhibit 10.3

When professionals have relationships with wealth management firms, the norm is to now and again make a referral. When they do make these referrals, it is no surprise if the wealth management firm is one of several such firms getting introduced.

What is most telling is that the clients are usually the ones who prompted the professionals to make an introduction in the first place. These professionals are rarely, if ever, going to do much follow-up after passing along the name of a wealth manager.

In stark contrast, advocates are squarely on your side and tremendously committed to helping your elite wealth managers succeed. They are exceedingly proactive in sorting through their clientele, looking for strong possibilities for your elite wealth management practice.

When these advocates refer their clients to your accounting firm's elite wealth management practice, they are not even considering any other firm. Also, advocates will make a concerted effort to ensure your elite wealth management practice and their clients connect.

The difference between having relationships with other professionals and having advocates is profound. So too is the impact on the overall success of your accounting firm.

There are a few key concepts that underpin building a pipeline of new high-quality clients from other professionals. Two of the most important ones are N.E.X.T. and the Law of Small Numbers.

N.E.X.T.: Pivotal to moving from dealing with just professionals to dealing with advocates is knowing when to walk away, referred to as N.E.X.T...

Never Extend eXtra Time

Many wealth managers find it difficult to walk away from another professional who could maybe, possibly, hopefully send them a single client. When the situation is not at all fruitful, many wealth managers say something along the lines of "any day now."

Elite wealth managers do not have any trepidation about moving on from a professional who is unable to provide the high-quality client referrals they are seeking. They know how to say: N.E.X.T.

The Law of Small Numbers: In researching extremely successful leading professionals who do a phenomenal job of creating a pipeline of new high-quality clients, we consistently find that while they have many extensive business contacts, they only have a handful of advocates. These advocates are the source of the most—sometimes all—of their new high-quality client referrals.

It is not the number of professional relationships that makes the difference; it is the quality of the relationships elite wealth managers have with a few carefully chosen professionals. The research reveals a striking fact. For elite wealth managers, five other professionals (at most) is the magic number. When wealth managers are working closely with more than five other professionals, the overall number of new high-quality client referrals they receive goes down most of the time. For each elite wealth manager, five advocates are very likely all he or she is going to need to achieve enormous success.

Discovery: The way these pipelines of new high-quality clients are built always starts with discovery. Elite wealth managers learn about other professionals through the discovery process. Only by extensively learning about the aspirations and obstacles, the perspectives, and practices of these other professionals can elite wealth managers help them excel. When these other professionals start to excel, they are on the way to becoming advocates.

During discovery, elite wealth managers gain a very solid and extensive understanding of the business models, the goals, the issues, and so forth of these other professionals. The elite wealth managers learn about their critical concerns and what they are doing to remedy the problems and overcome the barriers they are facing.

There are batteries of open-ended questions that enable elite wealth managers to learn about these other professionals, as well as find out ways to add value to their practices. The following are some questions elite wealth managers will often ask:

- How interested are you in earning a lot more each year?

- What services do you specialize in?

- How are you compensated at your firm?

- Where do you see your practice in a few years?

- How do you get new clients?

- How many clients do you have worth $10 million or more?

- Is there a particular type of client, such as business owners, corporate executives, or celebrities, who makes up most of your book of business?

Funneling: Elite wealth managers who have mastered discovery can often find new high-quality clients in the very first meeting, or within the first few meetings with other professionals. This process is referred to as *funneling*.

To engage in funneling, the elite wealth manager needs to first:

- Develop a deep understanding of the business model of the other professional.

- Learn about the professional's clientele, including how clients are usually sourced.

- Learn about the nature of the expertise the professional provides to these clients.

It is then possible for the elite wealth manager to identify possible clients for the accounting firm's elite wealth management practice, as well as for other accounting firm practices. Almost all the time, the other professional will readily provide information about clients so the elite wealth manager can find ways to add exceptional value. Funneling is also a way for the elite wealth managers to create opportunities for other professionals to earn more money relatively quickly.

Helping other professionals excel: To get a constant flow of new high-quality clients from other professionals, elite wealth managers are not only doing an exceptional job for their clients, but they are also helping these professionals excel. There are several ways to help other professionals meaningfully grow their practices, and none of these ways requires sending them clients.

One proven approach is to share the Everyone Wins Process. Doing so often results in these other professionals better understanding their clients, and consequently being able to deliver greater value to them. A consequence is that these professionals become considerably more economically successful fairly quickly.

Sharing the Everyone Wins Process turns out to be an extremely powerful way to empower other professionals, resulting in them having more highly satisfied clients, becoming more successful, and becoming advocates of the elite wealth managers. When elite wealth managers do a very good job of sharing the Everyone Wins Process, they are almost guaranteed to be introduced to a professional's best clients.

The way this works is having the other professional talk about some current clients, usually based on certain criteria. Importantly, the elite wealth manager does not want to know details about any of the clients being discussed.

By using the client version of discovery, and having the other professional answer the questions, most of the time, gaps in knowledge will quickly become apparent. In these gaps, there is often potential revenue for the other professionals. At the same time, the elite wealth manager is seeing if there are ways to deliver exceptional value to these clients.

Another approach that can help other professionals excel is to help them become thought leaders. We mentioned, in Chapter 6, that a thought leader shares ideas, concepts, and best practices without holding back. The intent is to raise the bar for everyone, especially clients.

Being a thought leader has a great economic benefit. Over time, being a thought leader results in more revenue through additional work with clients and new high-quality clients. Keep in mind that many professionals do not know how they can build their brand, and do not understand how they can be recognized as thought leaders.

By helping the professionals your elite wealth managers are working with to become thought leaders, those professionals will more likely become advocates of your elite wealth management practice and accounting firm. One powerful approach to help them become thought leaders is to provide expert content to these professionals for distribution to their clients, and referral sources can be quite powerful. There are many places to source expert content without cost. *Private Wealth* magazine (pw-mag.com) is one such source.

Conclusions

Although your elite wealth management practice is likely to be somewhat dependent on being introduced to the clients of accountants for growth, this is just the starting point. By adopting our methodology, your elite wealth management practice will end up with a steady stream of new high-quality referrals. You will probably have a steady stream of referrals that will come from clients and other professionals, such as attorneys and bankers.

When it comes to client referrals, instead of waiting for the phone to ring, the elite wealth managers will help clients understand whom to refer and how to refer. Taking such a proactive approach will regularly result in being introduced to preferred new high-quality clients.

Meanwhile, using the Everyone Wins Process, the elite wealth managers will be developing advocates. When other types of professionals become advocates, they will make a concerted effort to find high-quality clients for your accounting firm's elite wealth management practice.

By helping these other professionals do a better job—of becoming more proficient with the discovery process, for example—they will better understand their clients and regularly find new possibilities to be of service to them. A potent way to help these professionals become more proficient with the Everyone Wins Process is for your elite wealth managers to coach them on a client-by-client basis.

Also, helping other professionals become thought leaders usually results in more new high-quality clients for your elite wealth management practice. While the emphasis is on getting new high-quality clients for the accounting firm's elite wealth management practice, other practices at your firm will also greatly benefit. Very likely, these clients will have wants and needs that other practices at your accounting firm can address.

In the next chapter, we talk about converting your firm's elite wealth management practice into a family office practice.

CHAPTER 11

Building Your High-Performing Family Office Practice

IF YOU HAVE AN ELITE wealth management practice, you might want to "upgrade" to a family office practice. Just consider...

1. *How familiar are you with family office practices?*
2. *Why are so many accounting firms and other types of professional firms establishing family office practices?*
3. *What does or would your accounting firm's family office practice provide clients?*

Self-proclaimed family office practices are multiplying at an incredible rate. All you have to do, for instance, is look at all the many accounting firms that—on their websites—claim to have a family office practice. Or think about all the wealth managers that magically transformed into family office practices.

The truth is that for a great many financial and legal professionals, professing to have family office practices is nothing more than a marketing ploy. As there is no "official" definition of a family office practice, anyone can say they have a family office practice irrespective of the expertise they can deliver.

What is a Family Office?

The concept of family offices goes back to around the sixth century. At this time, each king and lord had a steward who was integral in the day-to-day management of the household and estate. The steward oversaw expenditures and the collection of taxes, organized large events, and was the head of court when his king or lord was away.

It is very likely that the family office concept arose even earlier, as the practice of trusted servants attending to the needs and wants of wealthy families reaches far back in time. Family offices became formalized, as individuals such as JP Morgan, Andrew Carnegie, and John D. Rockefeller created separate corporate entities to manage their wealth and deal with family matters.

Today, family offices are being described in all sorts of ways. But when you get right down to it, a family office is a very simple concept.

A family office is an expert coordinator of expertise that optimizes the lives of family members.

Some of the expertise is likely to be in-house, and much of it is probably outsourced. In researching family offices for decades, the most successful ones are extremely proficient at discerning the needs, wants, goals, and concerns of wealthy families. They are then able to connect these insights with high-impact solutions, producing exceptional value for these families.

The Growing Demand for Family Office Practices

The number of wealthy families is greater than at any time in history, and the amount and their level of affluence are greater than at any time in history. Moreover, the wealthy can be excellent clients for many professionals.

We believe the reason so many professionals say they have a family office practice is that, based on our research, the wealthy—defined as families with a net worth of US $10 million or more—generally prefer a high-performing family office practice to all other types of firms. For this cohort, high-performing family office practices are preferable to accounting firms with or without wealth management practices, law firms, private banks, wealth management and investment firms, insurance firms, and consultancies.

The appeal of high-performing family office practices is a function of the superior results the super-rich—who have a net worth of US $500 million or more—get from their high-performing single-family offices. Where elite wealth management can optimize the financial lives of families, a high-performing family office practice can optimize the financial lives and many other aspects of the lives of families.

In sum, what the wealthy want, and what your family office practice can likely provide them, are many of the same advantages the extremely wealthy get from their high-performing single-family offices. No doubt, wealthy families prefer having a high-performing single-family office. When that is not possible, the preferred option is a high-performing family office practice.

If you choose, you can take your elite wealth management practice and expand its offerings, making it a high-performing family office practice. It comes down to greater operational functionality, often predicated on a more expansive team of leading specialists. Mastery of the Everyone Wins Process is required with both elite wealth management practices and high-performing family office practices.

More than Elite Wealth Management

Your high-performing family office practice will add additional categories of expertise to elite wealth management. As the managing partner of an accounting firm, this is one of the categories your firm already likely provides—at least to some degree. Some other categories of expertise include:

- Administrative services
- Lifestyle services
- Family governance services
- NextGen educational services
- Special projects

Let us now briefly examine each category.

Administrative services tend to be very straightforward and often serve a critical role. They include:

- Dealing with all tax compliance matters including filing tax returns, audit defense, estate and gift tax execution, tracking, and administration
- Developing and updating the family balance sheet
- Producing income and cash flow statements
- Providing budgeting plans
- Bill paying and expense reporting
- Tracking and reporting investments including addressing cost and tax basis
- Bookkeeping

When it comes to administrative services, the high-performing family office is the chief financial officer for wealthy clients. Even though these services can be considered very straightforward, they can be very complicated and must always be executed well.

Considering you are the managing partner of an accounting firm, many if not all of the administrative services are available at your firm. Whereas some other types of professionals have trouble delivering these services at the highest levels, this is likely not a problem for you.

Lifestyle services are non-financial and non-legal services that tend to be very important to the segments of the wealthy. Of great concern to most wealthy families is receiving the best possible healthcare. Making this happen often translates into the high-performing family office practice connecting family members with the appropriate concierge medical practices, and monitoring the ongoing relationship.

Concierge medicine is an umbrella term used to describe several different retainer arrangements between a primary care physician and a patient. All the various forms of concierge medicine represent a return to privatizing primary healthcare. It is a way to get a higher quality of care where patients and their loved ones are center stage and stay center stage.

In many situations, the most critical benefit of being a patient of a concierge medical practice is the ability to spend time with the physician. It is not any version of assembly-line medicine, which has come to dominate many quarters of primary care. A high-caliber physician's ability to spend time with a patient means there is a stronger possibility that the physician will avoid errors, or the need to take shortcuts that might prove ineffective. Some of the services of many concierge medical practices include:

- 24/7, immediate on-call physicians

- Second opinion availability

- Complete case continuity

- Secure 24/7 access to medical records

- Access to leading medical specialists and medical centers

- Connected monitoring

- Leading-edge telediagnosis and treatment

- Destination medical planning

- Access to a foreign physician/hospital database

- Global medical evacuation

One service of concierge medicine that is gaining tremendous traction is healthspan extensions and longevity initiatives. They entail integrating cutting-edge wellness regimes, the most advanced healthcare capabilities, as well as alternative therapies with elite wealth management.

Family security is also extremely important to a large percentage of the wealthy. Their affluence can make them a target for criminals and the psychologically troubled. The wealthy often rely on family security firms to provide a range of services, such as:

- Property protection (includes securing houses and valuables such as artwork)

- Privacy and cyber protection

- Extensive background checks

- Personal protection

- Travel safety and security protocols

- Asset recovery

- Investigations of a business and personal nature

- Due diligence

The importance of family security is increasing at an alarming rate. The wealthy are looking for carefully chosen family security resources to help make sure their property is safe. Therefore, high-performing family office practices are taking steps to connect wealthy families with the best family security specialist that meet their particular requirements.

Another lifestyle service of interest to some of the wealthy is philanthropic advisory. While many of the wealthy are very clear about the causes they want to support, some are not that sure. Philanthropic advisors are engaged to help the wealthy with understanding their giving options and possibilities. Some philanthropic advisors will also get involved in monitoring donated monies. Concerning private foundations, for example, philanthropy advisors often assist with:

- Developing a strategic philanthropic plan including the foundation's mission, goals, and key initiatives

- Implementing the philanthropic plan such as issuing grants

- Engaging multiple generations of a family in the foundation's activities and board

- Determining appropriate compensation for foundation board members

Philanthropic advisory and charitable tax planning are different but complementary services. These two types of services habitually produce synergistic results. The aim is to make meaningful gifts tax efficiently.

Family Governance Services

Leaving the family business to heirs can be complicated. Many times, doing so is plagued by interpersonal conflicts that can destroy the business and the family. Your high-performing family office practice has the expertise to foster family cohesiveness.

Ensuring the intergenerational transfer of wealth and personal values, as well as the continuity of family businesses, requires elite wealth planning, combined with some form of family governance. By only focusing on the transfer of financial assets, these families are not optimizing.

Effective family governance often starts with delineating the family's history and values. Sharing the story of the family, and the way the business and wealth were created, can be quite educational for many family members, especially heirs who may not know important details.

For family members to work together successfully, their values, goals, and expectations must be aligned. This alignment helps them truly act as a family, rather than simply several people connected by blood with little else in common. To facilitate the family coherence that enables better decision-making, many families construct vision and mission statements for their family companies (Exhibit 11.1).

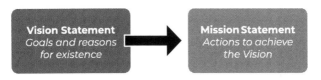

Exhibit 11.1

Another tool is the family constitution, which is a written document that details a consensus the family members have around core principles, values, and the long-term intent of the family. It is also a tool for avoiding serious conflicts and facilitating agreement among family members, by helping them constructively address their concerns and preferences. It can also set out the future direction and sometimes specific actions the family will take concerning the family businesses.

A key benefit of well-structured family governance is superior decision-making. When the tools of family governance are in place, there are relatively few missed opportunities, family hostility is minimized, and there is greater overall emotional calm. Moreover, the family business runs smoother and delivers better outcomes for family members and others, such as employees.

Family governance services are not only in demand by the wealthy with family businesses, but they are also applicable to many wealthy families, especially when these families are made up of several generations. Some accounting firms have the expertise in-house to provide family governance services. If not, there are specialists your high-performing family office practice can bring to the table and work with.

NextGen Educational Services

NextGen educational services take many forms. They are becoming increasingly fundamental to successfully preparing future wealthy inheritors to manage and lead in today's complex, increasingly transparent, hyper-competitive commercial landscape. Education that is transformative, issues-focused, and emphasizes reflective awareness is what future wealthy inheritors are looking for.

The requisite educational approach is geared intently around facilitating achievements. The focus of any viable educational program is to provide an extraordinary and highly actionable curriculum that will enable future wealthy inheritors to excel. Time is a luxury few can afford. NextGen educational services have to translate into accomplishments as fast as reasonably possible.

The following equation lays out the nature of NextGen educational services:

Applicable + Practical = Capable

Let us consider each of the components:

- **Applicable:** The educational content must be pertinent, relevant, and exceedingly appropriate to the issues, resources, and situations future wealthy inheritors are facing or will face.

- **Practical:** The educational content must prepare future wealthy inheritors to efficiently handle complex and conflict-ridden important matters, as well as enable them to take on the mantle of stewardship.

- **Capable:** By ensuring the curriculum is applicable and practical, future wealthy inheritors become quite capable. They will have the knowledge and skills, insights, and proficiencies to achieve high degrees of success.

Some accounting firms can develop and deliver NextGen educational services. Most rely on external experts working in conjunction with accountants or elite wealth managers.

Special Projects

Most high-performing family office practices engage in one-off special projects. Some examples of special projects include:

- Facilitating a cross-border adoption

- Buying an island

- Arranging for experimental stem cell treatments in a foreign country

- Overseeing the construction of a 60,000-square-foot mansion

- Arranging the paperwork and facilitating the process for admission to an extraordinarily exclusive private club

- Creating a life audit

- Supervising the forensic accounting work for a divorcing family member

- Arranging for a family member to be "disconnected" from a self-harm site and to then receive top-quality treatment

- Restoring the identity of a family member after her company was hacked

- Arranging for underage children to be extracted from a cult

This list of one-off special projects can go on and on. When it comes to special projects, external experts are almost always brought in, and the high-performing family office practice acts as coordinator and monitor.

The Role of Specialists in Family Office Practices

While your elite wealth management practice makes use of specialists, your high-performing family office practice would also make use of specialists—just more of them. Most of the time, the specialists you would need for your elite wealth management practice are the same ones you would need for your high-performing family office practice.

While the specialists required by most of the wealthy are easy to source, when it comes to the requirements of the super-rich, there are some super-niche specialists. While no services or products are truly unique or 100% exclusive in the private wealth industry, some astoundingly talented and experienced professionals are only accessible by other professionals who are "in the know." These experts are arguably some of the best at what they do, which is usually extremely specialized, such as:

- A prodigious musical theorist turned world-class professional poker player and Platinum Life Master bridge player (because he decided to spend his time in other pursuits) turned hedging strategist. He is concentrating on developing hedges for passion investments and geopolitical upheavals.

- A one-time juvenile delinquent (the files are sealed) who is currently considered one of the foremost experts on asset protection planning for multi-jurisdictional successful families. He is credited with helping develop or refine approaches like the "floating island strategy," which works amazingly well but often necessitates that the families are billionaires.

- A GO grandmaster who probably has one of the best track records for winning private trusts and estate lawsuits involving certain offshore jurisdictions. He tends to work for the estates but has been known to play all sides.

While most super-niche specialists engaged by single-family offices deal with wealth management, some address family conflict and family support matters. For example, a former stage magician and mentalist has become an outstandingly accomplished litigation and jury consultant. He is commonly engaged by one side or another when ultra-wealthy families engage in civil war.

There are also some exclusive boutique healthcare and family security providers. We knew a reclamation expert—through happenstance—who ended up being one of the top professionals when it comes to cult extractions. On the lighter side, there are the cryptozoologist, the cybernetic soothsayer, the quantum matchmaker, and the award-winning dollhouse architect.

Most wealthy families—including the super-rich—are unlikely to ever require the services of super-niche specialists. However, it is always nice to know they are available.

Conclusions

Retainer and project fees are commonly used to compensate the high-performing family office practice for these categories of expertise. Your high-performing family office practice is being paid to bring the best specialists to wealthy clients and make sure they are getting the best results possible. Some of these experts might very well be accountants, or even consultants in your firm.

If you are interested in working with much wealthier clients—most of them likely being business owners—then you might want to consider building a high-performing family office practice. If you have an elite wealth management practice, a high-performing family office practice can be thought of as an extension. Besides, you might already have all the expertise in-house to deliver the desired range of administrative services. Adding the other capability is often not much of a problem for many accounting firms, as you will probably be relying mainly on external experts.

One more consideration: by enhancing your elite wealth management practice to a high-performing family office practice, you will probably be able to attach and work effectively with significantly wealthier clients, including the super-rich.

If you want to learn more about family office practices, the online course—"Delivering Exceptional Value to the Wealthy: How to Build and Grow a High-Performing Family Office Practice"— is available at HNWgenius.com.

Reality Check

YOUR ACCOUNTING FIRM'S elite wealth management can be a game-changer. When conceptualized and implemented well, it can make a tremendous difference in the success of your accounting firm.

Let us review the promise of an elite wealth management practice.

- Optimizing the financial lives of clients
- Significant revenues from delivering exceptional value to clients, because of financial strategies and products provided
- Additional accounting revenues for accountants whose clients are working with the elite wealth managers
- More business for other practices at your accounting firm
- New high-quality clients, due to client referrals and referrals from other professionals, such as attorneys and bankers

To a large degree, it is up to you—the managing partner—to provide strategic direction and oversight for the promise of an elite wealth management practice to be fulfilled.

At the beginning of this book, we said loudly that the methodology we use and recommend is not for most accounting firms. We say this with a great deal of conviction, based on more than three decades of working with accounting firms that want to deliver exceptional and greater value to their clients—especially their wealthier clients—as well as become considerably more profitable.

If you are not *totally* in sync with the four core principles, our methodology is not for you. This means several things, including:

- The client deserves the best answers and solutions possible.

- Selling financial strategies and products is out of the question.

- Accountants must remain involved with their clients.

- Everyone has to be thinking about how each client solution will contribute to the short- and long-term greater success of the accounting firm.

We believe that for accounting firms to excel, when it comes to delivering financial strategies and products to clients, an elite wealth management practice is the answer. An elite wealth management practice is the marriage of state-of-the-art technical proficiencies with the Everyone Wins Process. Both are essential for any wealth management practice to be elite.

While we stand behind our methodology and believe it is the best approach, you may not agree. There are certainly other ways to approach delivering financial strategies and products to clients. And some of these other ways produce good results for clients and accounting firms.

We have seen accounting firms send out newsletters and reports about financial products and get some traction. We have seen accounting firm wealth management practices hold product-focused events and webinars that produce some business. We have seen wealth managers in accounting firms hold educational seminars for accountants that led to a few introductions. All these and other approaches can be effective to some degree. But we have yet to observe any of these different approaches come close to producing the outcomes you can achieve with an elite wealth management practice.

The difference between our methodology and these other approaches is in the level of business conducted, our intense focus on optimizing the financial lives of clients, and the extreme effort to make accountants far more successful, including helping them make their practices much more profitable.

The wealth management revenues generated with elite wealth management can be exponentially greater than the revenues generated by these other approaches. Then, you have to add in the additional revenues for the business sourced for your accounting firm's other practices. There is also the systematic addition of new high-quality clients introduced by highly satisfied clients and other types of professionals.

If an elite wealth management practice—as we have described it—is right for you and your accounting firm, please never forget optimizing the financial lives of clients and all the accompanying benefits that accrue to your accounting firm requires work. The methodology we use and recommend is not a secret—far from it. For example, most external experts are not hard to find and evaluate. The Everyone Wins Process is just the systemization of human nature. The discovery process is just the use of thoughtful questions driven by caring and curiosity.

For some accounting firms, an elite wealth management practice is transformative. Since there are *no* secrets, if you can implement it well, you can build and grow an elite wealth management practice. It is your choice.

About the Authors

Russ Alan Prince is the Executive Director of *Private Wealth* magazine (pw-mag.com) and Chief Content Officer for High-Net-Worth Genius (hnwgenius.com). He consults with family offices, the wealthy, fast-tracking entrepreneurs, and select professionals. He is the author or co-author of more than 60 books, including *Everyone Wins! How You Can Enhance and Optimize Business Relationships Just Like Ultra-Wealthy Entrepreneurs* and *How to Build a High-Performing Single-Family Office: Guidelines for Family Members and Senior Executives*. Collectively, the cache of research-based insights within Prince's publications is the most complete empirical analysis in the field and the largest, most comprehensive database on the topic.

Private Wealth Interview with Homer Smith

Bringing the Family Office Framework to Business Owners and the Clients of CPAs

For more than twenty years, **Homer Smith** of Konvergent Wealth Partners and the Integrated Family Office has been developing a client service model focused on guiding high-net-worth business owners from growth through the transition of their business and their wealth. He works extensively with accounting firms to help them optimize the financial and personal lives of their clients.

Russ Alan Prince: Tell me about your firm.

Homer Smith: Konvergent Wealth Partners was founded in late 2019 after I left a large broker/dealer in order to more holistically work with business owners and their key professionals. I met Paul Saganey from Integrated Partners, and he shared the same vision of building a more robust and collaborative relationship between CPAs and advisors to bring more value to clients. One of the key attractions to working with Paul was playing a key role in developing the Business Owners Solutions and Family Office practices at Integrated.

Over the last twelve years, I have been bringing many of the advantages the super-rich—families with a net worth of $500 million or more—receive from their single-family offices to families with a net worth of $20 million to $100 million. While there are many definitions of a family office, for me it is simply being the coordinator of experts that my clients need to optimize their financial and personal lives.

Prince: What's your role with clients?

Smith: My role is to get to know my clients at a deep level. I make a concerted effort to know everything and everyone that is important to them and how these people would be impacted by their decisions. In conjunction with my team of specialists, we identify the strategies and solutions that would meaningfully improve their businesses or their family wealth. I then make certain they understand the advantages and disadvantages of each proposed strategy or solution so they can make smart decisions.

For many of our clients—especially many of the wealthier ones—we are instrumental in enabling them to legally pay fewer taxes—both now and in the future. We work extensively with business owners in helping them either transition their companies to the next generation, or maximize their personal wealth when they sell. For just about all our clients, we assist them in protecting their wealth from being unjustly taken through malicious and unfounded litigation.

Prince: But wealth is also about making an impact. How do you help clients do that?

Smith: A large percentage of our clients want to make a difference in their communities or in the world at large. We show them how they can make a significant difference tax-effectively. To sum it all up, our ultimate goal is to help our clients optimize their financial world and many facets of their personal lives.

Prince: Growing a great business can be difficult for some advisors. Can you provide us with some perspectives on how you partner with accountants to deliver value to their top clients?

Smith: I partner with a small select number of accounting firms to deliver to their top clients, who are often far from super-rich, the same strategies and solutions used by many of the super-rich. Put another way, I work closely with accountants to help them identify opportunities to bring more value to their clients. My team and I empower accountants to identify strategies that could save their clients millions of dollars over time, better protect their hard-earned assets from being unjustly taken, help improve the value of their business, and get their business ready for sale when the time comes.

Our approach to partnering with accountants is to, first and foremost, make sure their clients are getting exceptional value. Secondly, the accountants have to earn significantly more. A powerful outcome of partnering with accountants is that they become substantially more successful. This takes several forms, including regularly and predictably being introduced to new clients for accounting and advisory services. Very importantly, we help our CPA partners build their own family office framework for their top clients.

Prince: A large percentage of entrepreneurs are likely to sell their companies over the next five years or so. What is the opportunity here?

Smith: In the next five years, many successful business owners will sell or in some way monetize the efforts they have put into their business over the years or even decades. At the same time, there is a lot of capital out there looking to be on the other side of those transactions.

While there is all this potential, we also know that most successful business owners do not end up highly satisfied with the outcomes of their sales. In reality, only about one in ten owners that complete the sale of their business say they were highly satisfied with the outcome. The reason for this is likely a combination of a lack of pre-sale corporate planning and pre-sale personal wealth planning.

On the corporate side, the business did not do enough to identify and reduce the risk in their business or to execute a consistent growth plan. On the personal side, they did not do enough tax planning to minimize taxes on the sale and into the future, as well as did not do enough to structure their estate to make it easier to create a family legacy and to protect the assets from financial predators.

Utilizing the expertise of the family office framework that we developed at Konvergent and Integrated Partners, we will give those business owners the best chance to end up with a highly satisfying exit from their business. The bottom line is that these successful business owners almost always end up with a lot more money than they would have otherwise received.

Prince: What do you see as the opportunities for accounting firms who are interested in working with successful business owners and the wealthy?

Smith: When it comes to business owners, the opportunity for CPAs to be in the middle of this historic wealth transfer is incredible. However, for many accountants, capitalizing on this once-in-a-lifetime opportunity is going to require making some adjustments to their practices. Also, with the burgeoning increase in private wealth throughout the world, accountants who can bring the family office framework to their top clients will have the best chance to remain in the "most trusted advisor" position that they have been in for years.

While, in many practice areas, accountants are under pressure, those accountants working with successful business owners and wealthy families who have adopted some form of family office framework are going to excel. Not only will they be doing a better job for their clients, but they will be generating significantly more revenues for their firms. They are also likely to find the competition has pretty much evaporated.

Prince: Is this approach right for all CPAs?

Smith: This approach is not right for all accountants. However, for those that want to grow their practice by working with fewer, wealthier business owners and families, the opportunities over the next five years can be a game-changer for them.

Private Wealth Interview with Paul Saganey

How CPAs and RIA Excel Together

For more than twenty-five years, Paul Saganey of Integrated Partners has been directing traffic at the intersection of financial planning, wealth management, and CPAs. Before founding Integrated, Saganey was a regional vice president for CIGNA Financial Advisors, a company that focused on providing fee-based financial planning services for the wealthiest clients within various wirehouse broker-dealers, and RIAs.

From the moment he launched Integrated in 1996, Saganey saw an opportunity for CPAs and financial advisors to work together. Partnering with financial advisors within the wirehouse community was the foundation for the Integrated CPA Alliance.

Prince: Tell me a little bit about Integrated Partners?

Saganey: Since 1996, Integrated has been helping financial advisors achieve their entrepreneurial vision by offering comprehensive business-building services, designed with the truly independent advisor in mind.

Prince: Was working with CPAs always part of the plan?

Saganey: You know, it's funny. From the beginning, we saw an opportunity to help support what a lot of people perceived as a financial advisor's competition: CPAs. We recognized that CPAs were getting licensed as financial advisors, and though they had a license we—and they—recognized that most CPAs were not prepared to offer fee-based financial plans to their clients, including business owners and higher-net-worth families, with complex financial lives.

Fast forward twenty-six years, and we are working with 150 financial advisors and 140 CPA partners who are presently servicing over $12 billion of client assets. Our CPA program is designed to pair advisors with CPAs to provide a consistent referral stream to access their ideal clients, and help move their practice up-market while providing enhanced services to the CPAs' clients.

For CPAs, the alliance provides three key differentiators to help them grow their firm: revenue sharing, strategic structure, branding, and awareness through marketing.

Prince: What's the vision from here for the program?

Saganey: I tell everyone that I have a twenty-five-year plan, but let's focus on the next five years. By 2026, Integrated plans to have 500 CPAs partnering with our affiliated financial advisors in a revenue-sharing, client-focused relationship.

Prince: Why would CPAs want to work with financial advisors?

Saganey: As we look ahead, we believe CPAs and financial advisors face three of the same big challenges: succession, depth of services, and technology.

- Should I develop young talent internally or partner with a larger firm?

- How can I meet the financial planning needs of my wealthiest and most demanding clients?

- How can I leverage technology and process-driven capabilities for maximum practice valuation?

The success of the Integrated CPA Alliance has been nothing short of extraordinary because it addresses these challenges. The program increased revenue by 25% just last year.

Prince: Stepping away from Integrated. Let's look at the industry. Where do you see the industry going?

Saganey: Change and evolution are the only constants in this amazing industry. For financial advisors and CPAs, the next three to five years will be the most exciting ever.

Financial stresses within the stock and bond markets, changing tax codes, and political posturing that happens right before our eyes every day are going to place our targeted clients in a position of financial uncertainty. When faced with an uncertain future, people with complex financial lives will search for advice and counsel that can be provided by only a small percent of the financial and accounting community.

This can all feel overwhelming. But for financial advisors and CPAs working together with their clients' best interest in mind, these changes mean "opportunity" not "stress."

Prince: What are the big hurdles ahead?

Saganey: When you blend this financial uncertainty with the fact that $7 trillion of wealth is being positioned to transfer to the next generation, of which much of it is small business wealth, you begin to see the future in a different light. The challenge is, how do you, as either CPAs or financial advisors, align your growth goals with the reality of your current situation?

There are three words I learned from Dean Jackson that we use within our organization to help advisors organize their thinking about the future: vision, capabilities, reach.

"The next three to five years will be the most exciting" is a bold statement. But when you think about it, for advisors that can look ahead—*vision*—and address the financial needs that invariably come from uncertainty—*capabilities*—the future will be filled with tremendous opportunities, especially when working with an invested CPA partner—*reach*.

The need for financial planning and wealth management will always exist, and therefore our industry has an exciting future. But remember, change and evolution is the only certainty. The definition of "advisor" and who provides financial planning advice will continue to change, especially for mass affluent clients. The compensation structure will continue to change, especially for mass affluent clients.

For high-net-worth and business owner clients, future competitors will struggle to service the needs of these financially complex clients. The expertise and planning flexibility required will eliminate the vast majority of "big box" enterprises looking for a piece of the financial services market.

At the end of the day, the future is exciting, but it's up to financial advisors and CPAs with their teams, and the partners in their inner circle to use their vision, capabilities, and reach to turn "exciting" into "opportunities." Success is a choice.

About *Private Wealth*

Private Wealth: Advising the Exceptionally Affluent is the premier resource for leading professionals focused on meeting the financial, legal, and lifestyle demands of ultra-high-net-worth individuals and families, including the super-rich (net worth = US $500 million or more) and their single-family offices. The cohort that comprises the exceptionally affluent is larger than at any time in history and is growing faster than at any time in history. A rapidly expanding majority of the exceptionally affluent, because of their substantial financial resources and often complex lives, require and desire extensive expert advice, support, and solutions to best achieve their desires and goals, and deftly address their concerns.

Private Wealth delivers state-of-the-art perspectives and insights on the exceptionally affluent and the leading professionals who serve them. The strategic and tactical content is fundamentally about delivering exceptional value to ultra-high-net-worth individuals and families. The information in *Private Wealth* can therefore be instrumental in helping leading professionals to build highly successful practices and businesses that—first and foremost—significantly benefit the exceptionally affluent.

Unique content is drawn from extensive practical experience and cutting-edge empirical studies. By design, a very sizable percentage of the content is highly actionable, enabling leading professionals to more powerfully connect with the exceptionally affluent, and more capably assist them to achieve their agendas.

While *Private Wealth* is primarily intended for the broad array of experts who desire to better connect with and serve the exceptionally affluent, based on our ten-year experience (2008 to 2018) with the print version, a sizable percentage of ultra-high-net-worth individuals and families, including single-family office senior executives, will avail themselves of much of the content. Because of the interest the exceptionally affluent have in the material, we are thoughtful about including content that will help empower them to more productively optimize their lives and the lives of their loved ones.

About High-Net-Worth Genius

High-Net-Worth Genius (HNWgenius.com) is the premier resource to empower leading professionals to meet the financial, legal, and lifestyle demands of high-net-worth individuals and families. In addition, there are resources available for high-net-worth individuals and families to help them increasingly optimize their financial and personal lives as well as the lives of their loved ones.

By delivering superior results, professionals can significantly—sometimes exponentially—grow their businesses. For example, the wealthy are steadily choosing family office practices over other types of providers. Being able to establish and methodically grow a high-performing family office practice results in greater value to high-net-worth individuals and families and considerably more success for the professionals.

At the same time, a large percentage of the wealthy, for various reasons, are being poorly served by the professionals they rely on. Many of the wealthy, for example, are working with Pretenders who are professionals that want to do a good job but are not up to the task. We provide educational resources to correct this and other failures so the wealthy can make smarter financial and lifestyle decisions.

Research insights, coupled with more than three decades of experience working with leading professionals and the wealthy—including the super-rich—produce actionable processes and solutions that can make a significant difference quickly.

Made in the USA
Middletown, DE
18 February 2023

25040545R00090